OLD AGE SUCKS

And Don't Give Me That Crap
About How It's Better
Than the Alternative

JAMES ROBINSON, JR.

Contents

Introduction

Eight years ago, I published my first book, *Fighting the Effects of Gravity: A Bittersweet Journey Into Middle Life.* The manuscript—about 15 years in the making—was a cute, rib tickler, a humorous group of essays which spoke to the trials and tribulations of midlife. Chapters included: "The Day My Butt Said Goodbye;" "Don't Cry for Me, Mr. Gravity;" "Oh, My Aching Body;" "Middle-Age Sex;" "The Agony of the Feet;" and my personal favorite, "They Call it Presbyopia, but It's Still a Pair of Bifocals to Me."

Though I began writing at age 45 (in the year 2005), I was inspired by an incident that occurred when I was 36, when a pair of my favorite jeans inexplicably began to fit differently, seemingly overnight. Never had I encountered such a phenomenon. My mind began checking off a list of both likely and improbable scenarios.

1. My trusty jeans had shrunk, having not been washed, and changed their shape in two-days' time.
2. My butt had become misshapen by some strange happenstance.

Conclusion: Levi's can't morph overnight; rear ends can. Midlife had hit me like a runaway freight train.

Ultimate Conclusion: My butt had fallen, and it couldn't get up.

Yes, a rump that couldn't stand up on its own eventually brought me to the realization that youth had gradually drifted off into the wild blue yonder of life, and that I would, one day, no longer do the things I could as a youngster. Little did I know that thoughts of death would also creep into my consciousness, my knees would get cantankerous, and my vision would begin to fail.

It was as if I had passed a sign on the road: "Welcome to Midlife: Keep Your Hands in the Car at All Times."

Since then, I've passed the middle-age baton to my children—ages 41, 39, and 38. They've grown to become amazing ladies. I couldn't be prouder. They have given me children who are a joy. I have written five more books—three fiction and two non-fiction. The novels deal with a dysfunctional family known as the Johnsons. One of the non-fiction titles features my father—a civil rights activist in the '60s and the first black to play football at the University of Pittsburgh. After he ended his stint in the limelight, he then hooked up with my mother, an educator, and began the task of educating the children of a little Pittsburgh hamlet called Manchester.

While I was busy fostering a burgeoning writing career, time snuck up on me like a crouching lioness, ears pinned back, surrounded by African brush, set to pounce on a gazelle.

Oh, there were the good years. My late fifties were a prime-time, cozy, comfy affair, a wind-up before the pitch, the calm before the storm. I could play mind games. I could pull out my trusty mental calculator and say, *"In 10 years I'll be 68 years old and in 20 years I'll be 78."* I could live with that. But those two decades would zoom by in the blink of an eye. Then, I looked up and I was 68. My mental calculator had turned on me. All of a sudden it was: *"In 10 years, I'll be 78. And in 20 years... well, let's not talk about that.*

I retired the calculator.

It had become clear. Middle age, that cute little butt-falling, Presbyopia-having, I-don't-want-to-dance, little fella had segued into the final act of life's little play. Old age was center stage, with all its rough and tumble evil intent. Old age—*The Last Train to Clarksville.* Remember the Monkees? Those were the days. Problem was, no one had bothered to mention it. And unbeknownst to me, I was right in step with the band. I was playing the *Notre Dame Fight Song* and didn't remember picking out an instrument or practicing the notes.

I did play clarinet all through grade school and high school.

It seems that, somewhere along the line, I was invited to march in this little parade and I accepted. There must have been invitations and everything. It would have been nice if someone had taken me aside and warned me.

My brain transitioned to the senior side of things, became enmeshed in those federally-funded programs called Social Security and Medicare—infamous budget gobbling programs designed for the elderly. And I was waiting for those massive entitlement goodies with open arms, like a bear stocking up on salmon for winter hibernation.

I was staring down the barrel of 70 big ones. My parents were 92 and 94. I was taking care of them. Waiting on them hand and foot would be more apropos. They handled their own breakfast but, after the Cheerios, my wife and I punched the clock. I often asked myself aloud, "Did I sign up for this?"

Well, no, but the answer was shrouded in mystery, one of life's, "Oh, didn't I mention this to you, dear?" moments.

Life elaborates: "Sorry, you must have been away from your desk at the time."

"You see, when parents live a long, prosperous life, someone has to step up and take charge of their needs, and since you're an only child, that someone is you. Suck it up, James, you little child. They can't live forever."

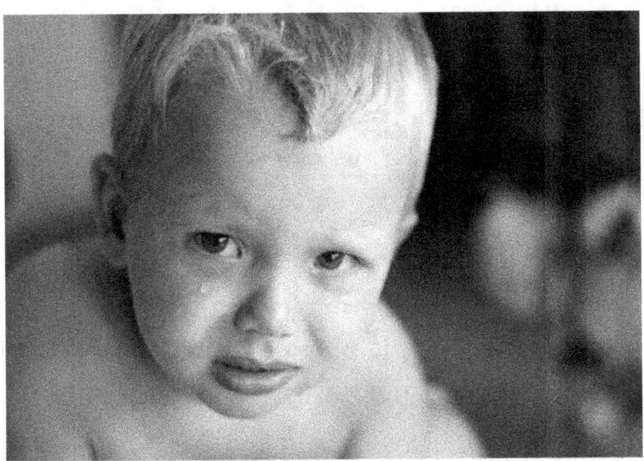

But that's a huge task. Especially when the so-called younger ones, charged with the care taking of the older ones, are slipping themselves.

Not long-ago, two-family friends—a mother and daughter—stopped by for a visit and the daughter asked me about the title of my first book.

I panicked; I had been working exclusively on this book and all I could think of was old age and it sucks and middle age and "these eyes" and cortisone. Gravity never popped into my head.

I stalled.

I thought it would come to me eventually, but it didn't. Oh, the blank look that must have taken control of my face.

"I can't remember," I said. How embarrassing.

She finally looked it up on her phone.

"Fighting the Effects of Gravity," she said.

It was obviously a warning sign: a blank spot in the o-zone of my mental landscape, a sizable chunk of brain cells gone forever, an Alzheimer's starter kit.

On the way home, Elizabeth, my antagonist's name, must have said to her mother, "I'm worried about Jay; he couldn't remember the name of his own book. And he's taking care of Rev. and Gram?"

Old Age Sucks isn't exactly picking up where *Fighting the Effects of Gravity* left off; it needed time to marinate, waiting in the wings like an actor delaying a stage entrance.

The third tier of life isn't warm and fuzzy like its midlife predecessor. Getting old isn't cute—some little blonde girl with ringlets and dimples. It isn't a little flirtation with aches and pains that steps up to your door, politely knocks and asks for admittance like a gentlemanly Bela Lugosi vampire in a tux.

"Goot evening. May I come in?" You'll have to imagine the voice.

If midlife is the middle-innings baseball pitcher, then old age is a ninth-inning closer with a 102-MPH fastball.

Old age kicks your door down like a jack-booted thug, grabs your neck and twists it, exorcist style, until your face is pointing toward your rear end, and then says, "There, that's better."

Am I exaggerating? Maybe. I'm still not considered what most people see as elderly. You know, walking with one of those walkers with a little seat. Just the other day a doctor looked at me and couldn't believe that I was 69. "Wow, I hope I look as good as you do when I'm 69," she said.

Call me cynical, but I see this as the ultimate left-handed compliment.

I used to get straight-up compliments like: "You're so handsome." Now the praise comes wrapped in a caveat. What this woman was really saying was: "When I get to your age, you'll be dead by then." Never mind that I was in the emergency room for cataract issues.

Then you get those "Hello, young man," greetings. I refuse to dye my hair so it's grey. I know they're not *really* referring to me as young. Young boys get called young men to give them the idea that they're more mature than they actually are.

"Want a lolli, young man?"

Is that what's next for me? Making a six-month, well-visit trip to my PCP, discussing my weight and having my vitals checked? Getting one of those bend-over-and-smile prostate exams? Then when all is said and done, "Want a lolli, young man?"

(Cue the laugh track)

But once you finish this book you'll understand what I mean. When you find yourself laughing and crying at the same time you'll say, "Hey, that guy's got a point."

1 Cortisone

or

Hell Yeah, I'll Take a Shot

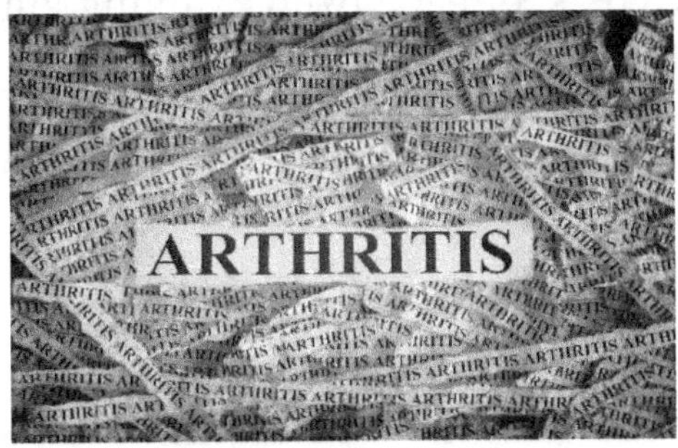

At some point in my lifetime, a group of wonderful people came up with the steroid drug and later cortisone—Edward Calvin Kendall, Harold Mason, and African American Percy Julian. There are two types of steroids: anabolic and corticosteroids.

You've probably heard of anabolic steroids. They're harmful to the body and are often used as performance-enhancing drugs for weight training and other athletics such as football, baseball, and track and field. Anabolic steroids used by weightlifters sometimes lead to "roid rage." Roid rage can look like this:

But older individuals don't have to worry about this type of behavior. We don't take anabolic steroids because our days of lifting heavy weights are over. So we won't get angry, fly into a rage, or get into bar fights. No, we turn to a corticosteroid medication that acts as an anti-inflammatory and gives us relief from swollen, inflamed joints. We want something to end the suffering of gravity's effects from walking on the earth for decade.

Our joints have had enough, and they're not going to take it anymore.

Medically speaking, as we age, cartilage located at the ends of bones begins to disappear due to decades of wear and tear, causing joint pain and stiffness. Inflammation develops. Many elderly suffer from osteoarthritis—shortened to arthritis.

Some misguided souls give arthritis the nickname "Arthur" and say, "Man, my Arthur is really actin' up. That Arthur is really something, ain't he?"

I prefer not to give arthritis a "sir name" because it turns a disease that causes millions of people pain and anguish into a nice old guy who dances like Mr. Bojangles (from the song of the same name), a gentleman I would invite into my home for a cup of tea and a biscuit.

Arthur happens to be an unwelcome friend of mine and, as I age, he's bouncing around my joints like wildfire.

Arthur is a mean son of a bitch. Arthur hurts like hell. I wouldn't want him marrying my sister (if had one).

I have arthritic, swollen knees that inflict excruciating pain every time I sit or stand. It gets to the point that if I rise from a seated position, especially a low chair or couch, I cry for help from my deity. "Oh, God," I say.

Sometimes it takes me two tries to rise from a seated position. I say aloud, "Double clutch," referring to the number of times you sometimes have to mash on the clutch to get a manual transmission into gear.

I say this not because I'm a car nut but because I'm a smart ass. I even had a raised toilet put in all of our bathrooms to make it easier to plop down and get up.

Sitting through a three-hour, super-hero movie makes me run for the aisle handrail to make a graceful exit after I've been sitting with my knees cooped up against the seat in front of me with no relief.

About halfway through a movie marathon I start to develop a little cinema-seat anxiety. *I need to get up and stretch my legs a bit,* I think. *But I can't get out.*

It's like claustrophobia for an arthritic.

My first post-movie steps must look like a toddler stumbling about, or an extra in a trailer from the new movie *Theater Zombies.* (Coming soon to theaters and streaming on HBO Max.)

Oh, the cruelty of it all. Can't an old guy go to the cinema? If I were a dog, they would label it animal cruelty.

Sometimes, I may brush past a swarm of other movie-goers to get to the balustrade. If there were a fire, I would probably knock old ladies out of the way to get to the exit.

I apologize to anyone I have injured in my haste to exit.

But wait!

There are movie theaters now with a row of luxury recliners that can be reserved online. Let's call them "old age doesn't suck so bad" seats. Plenty of room for people like me to stretch out. No anxiety. No need to run for the aisles.

God bless movie theaters. God bless America.

Knees have been particularly maligned throughout their existence. Beaten and abused over their lifetime, knees are ill-treated, forced to bend to a 90-degree angle and even to allow the femur to lie atop the tibia. Like this:

Now, that's just brutal.

The feet also take a pounding but they're not faced with such inhumane treatment.

When I was in my teen years all the way through my thirties, I was an avid weightlifter. I performed numerous heavy exercises including squatting with heavy weights on my shoulders—to build my thigh muscles.

It worked.

I built up my legs, but my knees paid the price. If my knees could talk they would say, "Remember those squats you did when you were young and full of vinegar, just so your legs could look big and masculine? You had testosterone to burn back then. Well, you're paying for it now. Just look at the shape we're in. We'll probably have to be replaced. May I present Exhibit 1."

And I would say, "Keep your exhibits. Knees should be examined, shot with cortisone and not heard; kiss my light-brown behind."

I see young people with healthy knee joints go into a squatting position and I turn my head and cover my eyes. I feel pain for them as if I were squatting myself. I say, "Oh my God, how do you do that?" Or, "I used to be able to do that when I was young."

They usually don't answer because they couldn't give a good damn.

When I was younger, I often heard the term "trick knee" used to describe a knee joint that gave out or slipped out of place. Oftentimes, an ex-athlete would attribute it as "an old football injury." I see the term used occasionally today. What we called a trick knee was probably, in fact, an ACL or meniscus tear that was never addressed.

Knees don't do tricks like the dog acts you see on *America's Got Talent*. Maybe you played a little game with your small child, throwing him/her up in the air and saying, "Uppie go." Well, knees can play little games too. As you walk about minding your own business, they suddenly give out as if to say, "Down we go." You can only hope they decide not to play their little game while you're walking down the stairs.

One step, two steps, three steps, "Down we go."

Hey, that's not funny.

And that goes for my feet, too. Planter fasciitis and arthritis (take your pick) have invaded my right foot. When I make a wrong move (or is it the right move?), sometimes in the vicinity of those damned steps, the foot caves in on me and I come up limping like a dog with an injured paw.

One time I held the door for a woman as I entered a drug store just as my foot gave out.

"Ah," I yelled with a pained look.

"Are you okay?" she asked nervously.

"Yeah, my foot just gave out," I said as I limped into the store.

When I paid my first visit to an orthopedic surgeon and had knee x-rays performed, I was surprised to discover I still have some vestige of cartilage between the bones, but my kneecap was loose and unstable.

I took some solace in the cartilage results but my orthopedist, who has a talent for breaking things down for his patients, informed me that if my knee were a tire with 50,000-miles worth of tread, I would have only 15,000 miles left.

"You won't make it to 80," he added. He meant 80 as in 80 years of age. Then he left the room. Hey, he's a busy guy.

I was then asked by one of his shot givers, "Do you want a shot?"

I said something to the effect of, "Yeah, sure. Why not?"

But what I was really thinking was, "Are you kidding me? Hell yeah, I want a shot. Do you think I'm here to get my tires checked?"

My back is also arthritic and gets stiff after sitting, standing, or bending even for moderate periods of time. Standing at the sink for too long washing dishes or just preparing dishes for the dishwasher gives me a backache.

Refer, once again, to Exhibit 1...

Allow me to explain.

Note how the calves are smashed against the thighs and both the calves and derriere are hell bent on touching the ground. Imagine the pressure this puts on the knees. Some might call this a "full squat"; I call it "He'll have to rise from this position."

Let's introduce the characters in this horror movie. I count six plates on each side of the bar, 12 in all. If I'm not mistaken each plate weighs 45 pounds. Add on 95 for the bar. By my calculations: 45 X 12 + 95 = 635 pounds. Hey, I'm not just a pretty face.

But standing in at number 2 ...

Behind the knees on the pain and wear-and-tear meter are the hips. Hey, when you think about it, how could anyone do those squats without the integral hips going up and down, carrying the load so your body can form a nice "L" shape?

When I was performing said squats, I never imagined that, one day, I would be describing myself as a letter of the English alphabet.

My right hip now gives out on me in certain situations like my beleaguered knee. I've even been flirting with using a cane.

I made the mistake of adjusting my father's cane to suit my height, just for the sake of reference, while he was looking. His response was swift and decisive.

"Hey, hey, hey." Then one big, "Hey! What are you doing? Don't be messing with my cane."

My pride has stepped in and made me leery of using any kind of walking aid. But then I say to myself, "Nobody cares if you're walking with a cane. It doesn't have to be an age issue. I could have been in a car accident. Yeah, thank God for accidents."

Huh?

Somewhere in the not-too-distant future, my right hip will require replacement, followed in short order by the left hip. It's not clairvoyance, I'm not a psychic. It's just in the cards.

I've simply had enough input from others in the same boat to be able to forecast my future.

"You'll be glad you did it," they say.

Yeah, whatever.

But I can't blame all of my disorders on the evil barbell. So, other than strength training, why does later life find me in this position?

Well, there were those everyday life tasks. The fact that I moved 12 times in my life certainly took its toll. I rented 24-foot trucks; moved refrigerators; dragged out washing machines, mattresses, bed frames, and huge couches—12 times.

I had a stable of friends in the ready and all I had to say was: "Moving."

"Oh, you're moving again," they said. "When? Where? What time?" I got the feeling that they never put their Jim Robinson moving clothes away.

But when we moved my parents out of their 1400 Pennsylvania Avenue mansion that they (and I for the most part) had been living in since 1965, all bets were off. That move, in November of 2017, was a two-day affair carried out by an honest-to-goodness, sure-nuff, reputable moving company.

I watched from the sidelines like a second-string quarterback sporting a microphone and holding a clipboard. It was like moving from the Ponderosa spread in *Bonanza* to a studio in Queens. But no Ben Cartwright, Hoss, or Little Joe for that matter.

Older brother, Pernell Roberts left that show in its heyday. That's principles for you.

When you live in a home with 7500 square feet of space and a seven-room basement for 50 years, you accumulate a lot of, let's say, stuff... and while I didn't lift much, I had to organize the... stuff. My parents, mainly my mother—my father had a militant, black leather jacket, a stylish afro, and four or five suits from a well-known Pittsburgh haberdashery—had two walk-in closets. They were, and still are, pillars of our community.

I, on the other hand, am no pillar. I walk in the shadows of the pillars. I carry the clipboard, I sing background vocals, I struggle to get a word in edgewise.

So, although I did no heavy lifting, I still had a heavy burden to move—sentiment.

The home had been a sanctuary for many over the years. Close relatives lived and died in 1400. My Aunt Vonda put up a valiant fight against cancer on our third floor for her final two years.

My grandfather lived a happy life playing his guitar in his cozy bedroom and feeding his birds from a second-floor kitchen window as he and my grandmother made a home on our second floor after he retired from the newspaper business. As his health deteriorated, I carried both my grandfather and my aunt down the long Victorian stairs of the mansion to their transportation to the hospital.

My grandfather returned to the house for another shot at life; my aunt didn't.

But after my grandmother died suddenly, my grandfather wasn't the same and I was there with the caretaker when he took his last breath.

On a lighter note, over the course of 50 years, my parents have received a lifetime of plaques, trophies, and sordid memorabilia. I didn't realize how much we-appreciate-you award booty they had amassed until I became the person entrusted with collecting it and moving it to another location.

I thought I was done at one point until I opened a door leading to a pantry off the kitchen. Three steps up to yet another room filled with odds and ends. Another space to stash fifty years of bits and pieces, this and that, whatever the hell, and who cares.

And, yes, more trophies, plaques, and *"In honor of what you did for your fellow man we're giving you this keep-up-the-good-work, swag."*

The move took two trucks, working two days, but it seemed as if we needed one lorry just to haul all of the tributes that had been bestowed upon the couple over the years. One award featured a light.

I guess they figured, "Better to see the awardee with..."

Don't cry for me, Argentina, but I won a couple of medals for writing contests that were misplaced during the change of venue.

I don't quite know how to put this but (whispering)... not every single one of the Robinsons' awards made the trip to the downsized digs. Some were lost or (gasp) misdirected along the way.

When it comes to my moving career, I make sure everyone knows my situation. I'm retired. I rest on my laurels.

Now when friends and relatives shift belongings from one place to another, I brandish my get out of jail free card. I quickly proclaim: "I don't move furniture, boxes, appliances, mattresses, box springs, or anything else for that matter." Not that they don't already know; they wouldn't have asked, anyway.

There are some privileges to being old and racked with pain and stiffness in my knuckles and hip joints.

I know I can't compare my twisted wreckage, that used to be viable, to the normal fingers and hands of elderly individuals in their eighties and nineties. I've seen their digits—mainly women—that look like this:

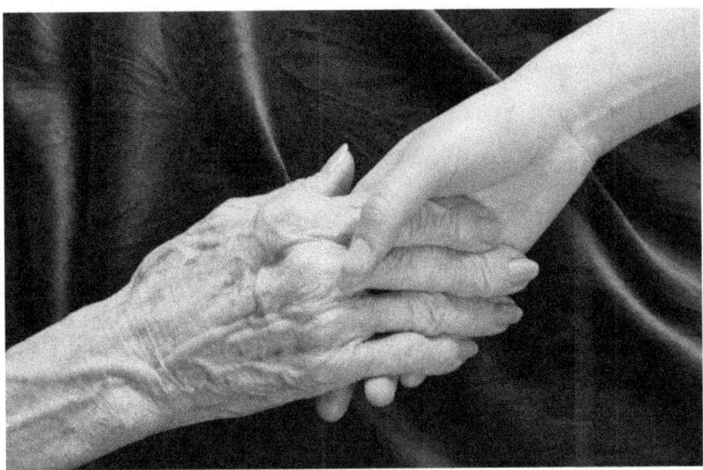

And I know that I'll probably never get to that point.

But knee replacement is a scant 15,000 miles on the horizon and the hips are not far behind.

But help is available for people like us. Cortisone is as popular and effective as Viagra is for sexual impotency. It doesn't cure arthritis, but it certainly put the brakes on it for a few months. Cortisone is injected into the joint like this:

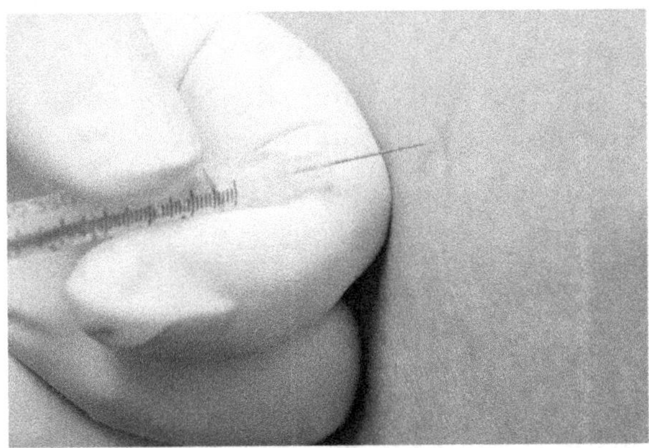

Does it look like it might be painful? Well, it is. But it's worth it.

Oh, I know what you're saying. "Boo-hoo-hoo." You're giving me the old get-out-of-here hand wave and chirping, "You're not old; you're only 69. You're a whippersnapper." Look at me. I'm on my second pacemaker. You know what they say… "80 is the new 65."

I always find it amusing when I hear stories about seniors who are still thriving despite advanced ages. "Aunt Gracie is 93, and still driving!" Yeah, right, but the question is, is she driving well?

My guess is… no.

Chances are, Gracie is ornery and none of her family has the guts to take her keys away. If the family would get together, hold an intervention, and even bring up the notion of commandeering her driving tools, she would cut them a new one.

She would say something to the effect of, "Sure, you can take my keys… from my cold, dead hands, bitch!"

Taking Gracie's keys would be an affront to her freedom. She would then have to summon Access or flag down an Uber every time she wanted to go to the market or get her hair done. No, Aunt Gracie will continue to endanger herself and others in her 1975 Plymouth Valiant with the statue of Saint Peter on the dashboard.

Gracie doesn't give a good shit as long as she can get around.

Trying to wrestle Gracie's keys from her just isn't worth it. Her loved ones wash their hands of the whole thing like Pontius Pilate symbolically rinsed his limbs of Jesus.

"You want Jesus over Barabbas, fine," he said. Shocked, he used the A.D. equivalent of a hand sanitizer. Then he gave them back their keys.

Gracie's family figures: "We tried. Everybody on their own."

Just hope you do not get in her way.

Well, to you people who want to play games with age I say, "How about kissing my light-brown behind?" Don't give me that *80 is the new 65, 60 is the new 45* crappola. Eighty is eighty and sixty is sixty. And how far can you go with that logic anyway? The next axiom I'll hear is "100 is the new 85." Only problem is, very few people make it to 100.

Anybody hear tell of death? How about "Death is the same old death"? Stop beating around the bush with the numbers. Stop tripping the light fantastic with the undertaker like those celebrity contestants on *Dancing with the Stars.* Sooner or later death is going to get us all. How about death is the same old, standing in front of a casket, looking down on a friend or relative, and saying: "Boy, doesn't he look like himself?"

Full of formaldehyde and dressed for the prom, he looks like himself? Yeah, if you say so.

Let's be real, here. We're primping and pimping out a dead dude. Like Elvis, the spirit has left the building. Do we have a car detailed before we send it to the junkyard?

But the truth is, there are good reasons why Gracie can still drive a car (as hazardous as she may be). We are living longer; we've got better healthcare. We've got doctors that specialize in injecting the magic numbing juice into elbows, and others who concentrate on juicing up the shoulders. Still more docs poke around in your knees and hips. And what do they specialize in?

They're the amazing people that introduce us to the magic of cortisone. Cortisone is the new *take two aspirin and call me in the morning.* Except you need a needle to administer it. And it hurts like hell.

My doctor's diagnosis and quick offer of treatment reminded me of my PCP who—during a recent check-up—asked how everything was going... "down there." I said things were going a little shaky—I had my ups and downs (tee-hee). "I can help you with that," he said quickly. "A little Viagra, maybe?"

The cortisone doctor prepared two needles—one for each knee—and then administered the drug. But the pain was undeniable. In fact, the little freezie stuff they spray on your knee to numb it before the shot even hurt like the dickens.

But after a few days, that wasn't so bad.

I know, we point to the exceptions. We see 70-year-olds running sprints and marathons. Well, some of us can hardly walk up and down stairs. We look at ourselves and see only big bellies and swollen knees. But we should keep things in perspective. It doesn't take long to realize those YouTube septuagenarians are genetic freaks. They make the rest of us look bad. If you're a non-hereditary mutant like me, you probably aren't running wind sprints. You're thanking whatever God you worship for whatever urge you have left.

In my case, I'm praising the good Lord and saying, "Thank you, Jesus, for allowing me to walk up and down these stairs. Thank you, Lord."

While others might say, "I get around in this wheelchair but at least I can get around," instead you'll say, "Lord, you blessed me with two artificial knees to get me around." Be happy if you can walk *with* assistance.

Or maybe it's, "I'm blessed with these five teeth. I can eat anything I want (although corn on the cob is off the menu)." Be happy if you have teeth.

Be happy if you have dentures.

In other words, there are varying degrees of blessings. I consider myself a spiritual, God-fearing individual and I've been around long enough to know the verbiage. Many thankful, God-fearing folks will end their phone messages with, "Have a blessed day."

When "have a blessed day" comes from a human's mouth over a digital cordless phone, it's like saying: *Don't take any wooden nickels.*

"I'm blessed" is a bit of a buzz phrase.

Blessed is another way of saying it could be a whole lot worse.

Great sentiment, there.

There's no doubt about it, I'm blessed. I have a great wife; beautiful, healthy kids and grandkids; and I don't suffer from any debilitating diseases. But in the complaining, bitchy, whiny grind we call life, I am breaking down like an old Ford Fairlane, heading for the great see ya later, alligator. I'm getting more screwed as the days go on. My joints tell me every day that their best days are behind them.

Consider: I can't lift a carton of milk from the refrigerator using my left arm without assistance from its right-side brethren. Such is the state of my left elbow, but this time I can't blame it on the evil arthritis. They call it tennis elbow—the insidious *lateral epicondylitis*—as opposed to golfers' elbow—the evil *medial epicondylitis*. Both conditions are caused by overuse or repeated usage of the elbow tendon.

Call me crazy. I used them during my 69 years of living to carry out life's little chores. As far as their namesakes go, there's no logic to it. I played very little tennis, and one game of golf in my life (unless you count the miniature variety). I have the lateral issues in my left elbow even though I'm right-handed. I would have to place the blame on the demanding bench presses I performed all the way up into my late thirties. The elbow is not made for such repetitive motions while prone with heavy iron plates on the ends of long iron bars.

Who invented such a thing?

When I was a big-time, lifting addict, I watched an avid group of bodybuilders about my age executing heavy bench presses and applying Ben Gay to their elbows as a pain deterrent. I doubt if they learned that from any of the medical journals.

I guess they considered it a preemptive strike.

I'm also guessing that no medical professional prompted them to take such a therapeutic course of action: *Just rub a little Ben Gay on your elbows before you lift. It won't do you a tinker's damn worth of good, but if it makes you feel better...*

Not to mention the fact that they smelled like my grandfather, I wager their medial and lateral ligaments are hurting about as much as mine are right now. Now don't they feel foolish.

Oh, I had those little aches and pains in midlife. But they were just annoying little signs of living that I accepted with a wink and a smile.

I didn't get shots for them.

The bad stuff laid in wait for 30 years and then ambushed me like a sneaky crocodile.

What's the solution? Although these maladies aren't caused by the malevolent arthritis, we can still count on the almighty cortisone to ease the pain.

Cortisone—a real shot in the arm. Ha, ha! Betcha didn't see that comin'.

Shots from an arm specialist to the medial and lateral areas provide the same relief. But it doesn't last forever. As a matter of fact, it has a shelf life of about six months.

Face it, people. Joints wear out. At some point, you may have to sound the alarm, smoke the joint, bring in titanium reinforcements, search the internet for a new kidney, procure a couple of new lungs, even put out a call for a new heart.

Just think of what they would have done for Chester with that wicked limp on the venerable *Gunsmoke* TV series.

I'm thinking a hip job or two may have done the trick.

Or not.

But Chester was born in the wrong century. The Wild West was too wild for swapping out hips.

And that was too bad.

Can you imagine what it was like to ride a horse all day herding cattle or to get from one town to another? No doubt about it, the Old West needed orthopedists.

Do what you have to do to make yourself as comfortable as possible in your later years. Trade in your old joints for new ones if that's what it takes.

Get a shot. Take a pill.

Remember, cortisone is your friend.

2 These Eyes
and the Mystery of Third Eye Blind

In 1969, a rock group named The Guess Who dropped a song entitled, "These Eyes." I recall the rhythm being one of those catchy tunes that becomes an "earworm"—implanting itself in your head for days.

But I never thought that 50 years later it would become my mantra.

My 92-year-old mother feels the pain of arthritis in her knee and says, "Oh, that knee," as if the appendage is not part of her body. I feel a little strange comparing myself to a woman eight years removed from the triple digits, but when my vision continues to act up, I find myself saying in disgust, "Oh, these eyes."

In my middle-age years, I hung out around the internet's own Professor Google and stumbled upon a new word—presbyopia. Presbyopia, I discovered, is the proper word for the condition which causes us to hold reading material as far away from our faces as possible. Technically, it's farsightedness due to loss of elasticity in the eye, making it harder to do up-close tasks.

Wow, that makes me sound educated.

In reality, you have to buy "readers" or bifocals to see up close.

It's a problem that usually crops up in middle-age. I wrote about it in *Fighting the Effects of Gravity*. I was around 45-50 years old when presbyopia and I crossed paths. But I had heard all the hoopla. I knew it was coming.

I already wore corrective lenses so I just visited my optometrist. Having clicked those lenses up and down for hours—you know, "Which is better... 1 or 2, 2 or 3, 3 or 1"—she rolled back in her chair and delivered the bad news, "James, it's time," like a jail guard summoning me for a trip to the room for lethal injection.

"Dead man walkin'!" they say in the movie of the same name as the convicted killer is escorted for a triple-header—a humane euthanasia with Jill Sarandon at his side, a civilized, three-part death cocktail.

Since I already wore glasses, I ended up getting the no-line bifocal. I could be vain and hard-of-sight, too. In this case, poor vision—corrective spectacles, that I was forced to wear all my life, a bane to my existence—were my savior.

Yeah, I know, vanity run amuck.

This way, I could hide my visual insufficiency, and no one would know I had presbyopia, while those with otherwise good vision who developed the wicked far-sightedness had to find a place to store up-close readers.

And how obvious they were. What do you do with glasses that you don't wear all the time? With 20/220 vision like me from the time you were in grade school, glasses were as permanent a fixture to my face as the nose they sat on.

When I was younger and girls were describing me they would say: "Oh, he's cute. He's tall, dark, and wears glasses."

The fact that there were people running about who had to find a place to stash their part-time glasses didn't escape my little brain. I saw those individuals who had reached the world of readervillle wearing half-glasses down on their noses and I knew why. These spectacles were performing double duty— look down to see that wicked small print, look over them to see life in the big-boy world.

It's not an attractive look.

Then there are those long chains that midlifers wear around their necks so they can call upon glasses when needed. Requiring readers is like hiring someone who works every other hour, like having a husband or wife you summon only on certain occasions.

"Honey, I need you to cook me dinner, now. Then you can go away for a while."

"I need you for sex now, sweetie. Then you can go back into my purse."

I promised myself that I wouldn't be caught dead with one of those chains strung around my collar.

As I aged, however, problems with my eyes grew. Issues that weren't just normal, run-of-the-mill matters began to crop up. At 65, the same optician informed me that I had developed cataracts.

"You're going to have to get those taken care of, James," she said. "No hurry."

My eyesight may have been diminishing but I could certainly see my future.

"Damn-near, blind man walkin'!" would be the charge. Only this time we would renew acquaintances.

"Haven't we met before?"

Cataract surgery didn't seem like a big deal. No one shared horror stories. No one came to me and said: "Do you have a living will? This is going to be a terrible experience. My cousin had his cataracts removed and he hasn't been the same since. Now, he has a cane and a dog and collects disability. The dog is really nice, though."

I picked my doctors and their pamphlet gave me a choice of two surgeries: laser or scalpel. Laser—a thin beam of light that slices through its target like a hot knife through butter. You know, Captain Kirk leading a group of men to a strange planet: "Lasers on stun."

Or so I thought.

Seemed the ideal way to go; it sounded neater and cleaner and safer. A scalpel involves cutting. Scalpels slice open flesh prior to surgery. Coroners slice open bodies with scalpels prior to autopsies then go about their business of weighing internal body parts and... No, thank you. Who wants someone cutting on their eyes with the same instrument used for slicing open dead skin?

However, health insurance companies don't share my vison (no pun intended). Cash has more to do with cataract surgery than you might think. My Medicare and Medicare Supplemental would only pay for the basic scalpel cataract removal. Laser surgery would cost $1500 more per eye.

I could almost hear the Medicare Boys saying: "Okay, we'll pay for the basic scalpel procedure but that's it. You're footing the bill for the high-tech stuff, Mr. Flash Gordon."

Then came the litany of upsells and extras. For laser surgery restoring 20/20 vision that will require only readers, an additional $1500 an eye. Laser surgery with perfect vision that needs no readers, $3000 an eye.

It was like the sticker pricing on cars. Air conditioning, power windows and brakes come standard. But if you want a sunroof, heated leather seats, all-wheel drive, and USB ports front and rear it's going to cost you an extra $3,000.

I opted for the $1500 package with readers. No leather.

As I went through the prep work on the day of surgery, I kept throwing in one little joke—or a variation thereof—with each person I came to. "Left eye, blind… Right eye, blind…"

Obviously, a reference to Third Eye Blind, the American rock group.

I couldn't get a laugh. Tough room.

But when it came time for the procedure, there was this wicked truth that became apparent. Things would not go as planned.

Contrary to what Gladys Knight may have said, the Midnight Train got derailed prior to its arrival in Georgia. The laser never showed.

I'd like to tell you that I saw a laser show, that once my eyes were numbed up, lights began flashing.

But they didn't.

Perhaps the lights were a little dimmer than I thought they would be.

Not likely.

Perhaps, like a Broadway Show where the star can't go on and a stand-in takes their place, the laser procedure was a no-show, and a second-string method was summoned from the bench—not as talented as Mr. Laser and ugly as hell.

It was a real kick in the tail. Like paying to see Sammy Davis Jr. and getting Ethel Merman.

"Get in there, and win one for the laser," they said.

The replacement procedure was a crude fella. A contraption was placed on the eye—not painful, but the pressure was wicked. It was one of the more uncomfortable feelings I've ever experienced.

My best guess is, with the stand-in, cataracts are broken up like a meteorite in one of those "the world is ending" movies.

But that's my guess. I have asked a lot of credible eye experts since who have yet to render an opinion or offer a good explanation. Just a lot of blank looks.

Just let me say, without casting aspersions on any doctors or medical organizations, that I got fleeced.

As the Beatles once said, *"I should have known better."*

I should have known that when someone gives you a sheet in your packet that looks like a menu from Dairy Queen that something is amiss.

I'll take a bullshit Oreo Blizzard please, hold the laser.

Sure thing. That will be $3000.00.

Did I get rid of my cataracts? Seems so. Was my natural lens replaced with an artificial Multifocal IOL lens? Beats the hell out of me. Did I get an eyeful of retina tears and displacements and heartache for two years after my *hey, what the hell is that you're putting on my eye?* I'm guessing, hell yes.

Hey look, old age sucks enough. I don't need a second-rate, stand-in cataract system ruining my eyesight.

I paid for a light show, and I got a shit show.

Captain Kirk, where were you when I needed you? Your lasers were definitely on stun.

My new chant is, look before you leap. What's wrong with a scalpel? Scalpels are good. Scalpels, in the right hands can do wonderful things.

Old age sucks. But I shoulda known better.

3 So Long, Libido:
It's Been Good to Know Ya'

Libido—also known as sex drive. That's a good term for it because it's the libido that drives off in the middle of the night and leaves you in the lurch, like when owner Robert Irsay packed up the Baltimore Colts in the early morning hours and hustled them off to Indianapolis without bothering to tell the city and its fans.

After the hasty exit, bumper stickers in Baltimore read, *Will Rogers never met Bob Irsay.*

Ouch.

Baltimore did get the last laugh, however; they were awarded another pro football team (the Baltimore Ravens) when Art Modell packed up the Cleveland Browns—this time in the daylight—and moved to Baltimore. To rub salt into the wound, Baltimore went on to win a Super Bowl.

Has it been so long ago that my hormones were raging, my libido was off the charts, and erections were all too happy to come out and play at a moment's notice?

Sometimes without any notice.

My friends and I would sit in high school class and get erections for no apparent reason. We didn't even have to look at our female classmates (although we did a lot of that, too). Just having male genitalia was enough. Our guys were ready, willing, and able to prove themselves.

"I'm here if you need me, James," Little Jimmy would say. "I won't let you down, sir." (No pun intended.)

"Not now," I would nervously mumble, "the bell is going to ring."

Why was Captain Penis so anxious? Because I was juiced, I had an abundance of libido, a sex drive that just wouldn't quit. My little teenage hormones had plans for me. I was a ruthless procreation machine.

Down, boy.

My sex drive was working overtime for me to have intercourse. I can visualize it like Scotty in the *Star Trek* movies, only this time he had a cocky grin on his face, "Captain, I can give you all the power you need."

Just as tigers, lions, and other animals in nature fight for territorial rights, and ultimately the best mating privileges, my friends and I were being set up for finding the best females for mating.

Yes, we didn't know it at the time but there was a conflict raging. We guys were giving in to our sexuality. We were thinking of the pleasure and the mystique of sex and just having our initial sexual encounter.

Girls were thinking, "I'm not going to get pregnant, you horny asshole. I'm going to college."

However, little did we know, our bodies had something else on their agenda. Our physical selves were staking out territories, preparing for procreation. We would have urinated on grass and trees but that just wouldn't have been appropriate. The dialogue went something like this:

Teenager: "Wow. Check her out! She's hot. I'd like to make out with her (terms changed to protect the prudish)."

But our libidos were saying: "I'm just setting you up for the kill. Flap your beautiful, colorful feathers around like a peacock, and show off your physique to the ladies. But this isn't the time for mating; you'll ruin the course of things."

If we happened to mix the two (excitement and procreation), we were usually headed for trouble.

Consider that one of my 16-year-old friends did jump the gun and impregnated his girlfriend. An hour or so of intense foreplay led to a hot minute of sex and two lives changed forever. A condom, what's that?

My guess is, after the heavy breathing was over, they looked at each other and said: "Uh oh, what have we done?"

As Peggy Lee once asked, "Is that all there is?"

My best friend came to high school one Monday morning wearing a wedding band that he hadn't been wearing the Friday before. My classmates were horrified. "Bobby," (name changed to protect the innocent) "is married," everyone gasped. I paid a visit to him at his locker and he calmly flashed the nuptial jewelry.

No mystery there. Bobby was trying to keep it together. As my father would say, "Trying to play a crooked game, straight."

This incident took place over 50 years ago, when girls didn't just have babies and go merrily on about their way. I wasn't there for that fateful weekend when my friend and his girlfriend found out that they were with child but I can pretty much figure out the discourse.

There were tears and finger pointing amongst the two families, with plenty of blame to go around. Much ado about the girl's honor and how my friend was going to marry her as soon as possible to make an honest woman out of her. Because it was obvious that, by their standards at least, she was as dishonest as hell.

"You two were old enough to have this baby, so you're old enough to get married and make it legal," they said. Apparently, having a child out of wedlock qualified for a jail sentence. The girl should have been sporting an ankle bracelet.

Bottom line: there would be no *Scarlet Letter*, here.

Meanwhile, my friends and I were, to borrow a modern-day phrase, lame as all get out.

Most of them, including me, were virgins.

A good porn flick would probably have sent us into orbit.

Those who weren't still virgins lied like 8' X 10' Oriental rugs about sexual encounters.

According to them, all of their hook-ups lasted for hours. My married friend did stick a pin in this bubble by honestly proclaiming: "Don't believe that stuff about sex lasting for hours."

One of my good friends, now deceased, sent for a kit to make wine. But none of us ever thought of procuring a porn flick. Were there none available in 1970? We did manage to get into a semi-raunchy movie once.

As I got older, my libido raged on and my male member continued to offer assistance. I got married at 24, began having children at 28. But at 30, with my wife at 25, she required a hysterectomy which meant no more children. It might be interesting to note that her gynecologist told her that once he performed the operation, he, in essence, would remove the baby carriage and leave the play pen.

What a jokester.

Obviously, our days of having children were over. But Mr. Libido and his sidekick the ever-active penis didn't get the email. We were free to explore new worlds, to go where lives ruled by condoms, diaphragms, and sponges couldn't go. They lived on with a few new wrinkles from us.

Porn movies—or as Dr. Ruth refers to them, explicit sexual material—spiced things up a bit. But there was nothing terribly drastic—no handcuffs, whipped cream, or whips and leather.

Chandeliers swinging from the ceiling would have been my demise.

There were no libido-led mutinies throughout my thirties, forties, fifties, or even early-to-mid-sixties. But it was at this point that old age began to creep in with its *turn out the lights, the party's over* mindset. Call it what you will, but it looked an awful lot like something big was about to come to an end.

1. So long, slavery

SIGNING THE EMANCIPATION PROCLAMATION.

2. Don't call me; I'll call you

3. Think you were going to live forever?

Ba-deep, ba-deep, ba-deep, ba-deep, that's all folks!

One night with no warning, my libido turned in his letter of resignation. Actually, that's not quite accurate. He announced that he was going from full-time to part-time. He just didn't bother to consult me or give me his time sheet.

For my part, I refused to provide him with a letter of recommendation. Guess I showed him.

You would think I would have gotten a note or text, postcard, email, Instagram, or something from the ingrate. I thought we was boys.

His answer would have probably gone something like this:

"First of all, stop trying to be ghetto. Your heritage says you are 45% European. I saw your 23andMe results. And we wasn't boys.

"Secondly, in case you haven't noticed, you're old. You have officially reached the landmark title of Old Age. Middle Age ends at about 50. Where were you? It was in all the papers. Perhaps you forgot when you signed up for Social Security at 62 (I would have waited, by the way) and Medicare at 65. Nothing lasts forever. Look what I have to work with. Your prostate sucks. You better get that fixed, by the way.

"I'll have one of my associates stop in from time to time. It's been fun. We had a good run, didn't we? Gotta go."

Leaving on a jet plane like John Denver. Love that song.

See what I mean?

The bastard.

Of all the nerve. One second he's there; the next he's gone. Leaving me in the lurch. A little heads up would have been nice. And where's he got to go, anyway? Such a busy agenda. Something better to do? Card game? Good movie on Netflix, Showtime, or cable? Got to set up the Ouija board?

No, he's going to leave some other guy in the lurch—another unsuspecting bloke lying on his back with a deer in the headlights look on his face, saying, "This has never happened to me before. I'm not a man anymore."

His wife or significant other will offer reassurances: "Oh, don't worry. Everything is going to be all right." But in reality, they're thinking, *Oh, crap, here we go.*

It was a cold, heartless act. Like a boyfriend or girlfriend breaking up with their mate via text, a wicked cruise missile fired from long range. The least one person can do for another is to offer the standard line, "It's not you, it's me," face to face.

You know that line about marriage, "You have to work at it"?

Okay, I'll buy that one. Marriage is a tough nut. But when the actual act of sex comes easily for almost seven decades and then goes on the fritz without so much as the *thump, thump* warning of a flat tire, it's a real shock to the system. I'm waiting for someone to say to me: "Sex is good until you get to be our age, then you have to work..."

Whoever this person is that was about to make this statement was unable to finish because my fist was down his throat.

Talk now, bitch.

I'm in shock. I don't want to brag or anything but I was pretty good at this act for 40 years. Then somebody just yanked the plug out of the wall like a toaster plug after the toast is done.

I'm not working at anything. I'm not a big fan of the little blue pill and I'm certainly not going to get whatever pump I hear tell about being installed wherever it gets installed. I'm not going to turn my sex life into a bicycle tire.

I'll watch some soft porn on a risqué cable station on a Friday or Saturday night just to get some vicarious thrills. I'll say, "I used to do that." But then I lose interest. "Enough already."

Sometimes my libido will put in a cameo appearance, come back for a brief visit, pretending to want to get into the action, getting things all stirred up, and then surreptitiously creep out of the room while I'm studying the action.

Bastard.

My wife seems to be just a little too happy that my run is ending. Fact is, I think, given her druthers, she would prefer a good night's sleep. I suppose many ladies would. However, most of them enjoy the roller coaster ride once that first dip starts, after the bar swings down.

And if I'm to be totally honest, she's mentioned the sleep preference thing to me on several occasions. Fact is, when I mention to her how lucky she is that, sexually, she probably won't have to be bothered with me much anymore, she emphatically whispers, "Yes," under her breath and gives an energetic Tiger Woods fist pump just beyond my peripheral vision.

But I know she's kidding. She is kidding, right?

Not that it hasn't been this way for the past few years.

The bottom line is, you miss the guy for more than just the sexual act. I miss all of the rigmarole that used to go along with sex. You know, the rituals, pre-game warm-ups, the little dances, shows, and appetizers that we guys go through to get the party started. Like the unknown rock band that warms up the audience for the Rolling Stones.

Like rubbing two knobby sticks together.

I miss the thought of it. The anticipation.

It's a guy thing. I'm thinking, *This would have been a night when I would have been planting hints.* "Hey," I would risk, "what do you say to a little..."

I was usually the one rubbing the two sticks together.

Amazingly enough, I was still a little shy to bring up the subject. After 45 years of asking, or hinting, I was nervous. What did that say for me?

Well, I'll tell you what it said. It said that it was little wonder I never scored as a teenager.

I went on a date with a young lady I worked with over a summer off from college when I was about 18. We went to see the original *Superfly*—the big movie at the time—that boasted an extremely hot sex scene. When I took her home she quietly asked me if I wanted to come in.

Ah, yes, the magic words. I didn't catch the inference.

There wasn't much to do on my part. The table was set, the meal was cooked, *Superfly* had stirred the pot. Hey, it wasn't like I wasn't hungry. But I had no idea how to seal the deal.

During the evening, she actually yawned. A warm goodnight sent me packing.

In my defense, she had already been married and separated from her husband, and I was a total babe in the woods.

There would be no second date.

She was, as they say, hot to trot. I hadn't even had dance lessons.

I haven't watched *Superfly* since.

There was that remake with Samuel L. Jackson and Vanessa Williams but... not the same.

Well, to my timid request for whoopie I might get: "We'll have to see, I'm really tired." Or, "I may have to take a raincheck. I'll see you tomorrow." At least I never got that "Not tonight, I have a headache" retort—a line so impersonal, trite, and overused it could be texted or emailed, or written on a notepad and held up like a cue card.

Raincheck? Well, it was a sweet refusal, a warm raincheck but a raincheck nonetheless. Let's be real, rainchecks are for baseball. You do realize that when a baseball game is rained out, the fans get a "raincheck" to see another game.

Sexual rainchecks sort of ruin the mood. I'd lie on the bed thinking about my raincheck and watching SNL. *How about that? Alec Baldwin is guest host again.*

All dressed up with nowhere to go.

But I got over it. Also, and this is my own fault, my wife and I slept in a queen-size bed for years. A queen-size bed made her a captive audience. The area to sleep in was so small I could attack from behind and there was little she could do.

Other than smack my hand and fall asleep.

But as we grew older, sleep took preference over fun time. We wanted more room for sleep so we opted for a king-size bed. Little did I know that, when it comes to coitus, king-size beds are the devil's workshop. Oh, they give you more room to sleep. But there is so much distance between two sexual partners that I damn near had to call an Uber to reach paydirt.

Okay, maybe that's pushing it.

You know, cheetahs are fast, but gazelles can get a head start while the lean, spotted, speedy cats have a lot of ground to cover to catch their prey.

But hey, I'm happy for the space these days. What with my sleep apnea and all. I started off with a CPAP machine and one of those jet-pilot masks, but that proved too cumbersome. The masks got smaller and smaller but I could never adjust. I've finally ended up with an oral appliance which manages to push my bottom jaw back and help to keep my airway open.

I think the problem is with the sex act itself. Sex is just too pleasurable for its own good. Sex should be boring, unimaginative, damn-near painful.

Sex should be for procreation. And that's it.

"We want another kid," we should say. "Let's try for a boy. I guess we have to... copulate."

"Doggone it. Let's get it over with."

One thing is for sure, there would be no accidents, no need for birth control, no premarital sex. Why should there be talk of G Spots and orgasms? Why should there be magazines that tell women how to make their husbands scream so loudly they'll wake the neighbors?

Now into my later years, there wouldn't be much to miss, would there?

But we aren't built that way. God and his administrative assistant, Mother Nature, had their reasons for allowing us to enjoy ourselves during procreation. It's called intimacy—an important part of the human experience. And we humans ruin it like we ruin everything else.

We waste it, we forgo it, we brutalize it, we cheapen it, and we dare to call it a friend.

So, as Bob Hope once said, *"Thanks for the memories."*

So long, libido.

So long, intimacy.

So long, anticipation.

Goodbye, queen-size bed.

Hello, king-size bed.

Goodbye, rainchecks.

Goodbye, SNL.

Goodbye, Alec Baldwin.

Good Night Moon.

4 When Children Have Children the First Grandchild

There are two ways to look at the title of this chapter. The first way to see it is that I'm about to discuss the tragic topic of young children, perhaps still in their teenage years, having children. Children having children. Children who can barely take care of themselves having to care for someone else. Babies having babies. Girls who end up behind the eight ball because oftentimes, the father has flown the coop like those swinging doors in the cowboy saloons. Children who...

Okay, enough. You get the idea.

But why would I enter into this subject? This book is about old age and how it's affecting my life. I told you that from the beginning. So why would you let me trick you like that?

You see, my daughters now range in age from 39-42. They all had children after they were married and settled into their lives.

Well, now that I think about it, there was my middle daughter, Erin, who walked down the aisle at age 29 carrying my grandson, B.J. No, she didn't physically carry him in her arms; she was pregnant with him at the time.

But there was no shotgun wedding. There is no stigma now surrounding women who bear children prior to marriage. She simply wore a maternity wedding gown. And she was beautiful.

When I speak of children that they have bestowed upon me, I speak of my adult children having grandchildren—those little creatures that your seedlings bestow upon you—creating another generation.

Robinsons having Robinsons. Even though they might take on another last name... or two.

Since my wife and I produced three girls, the Robinson name is kaput, headed for extinction like the T Rex.

Part of old age and passing your seed down to another generation is the grandparent name change. I didn't officially change my name on my birth certificate and driver's license, but I may as well have; names are changed when you have grandchildren whether you like it or not.

For the most part, you like it.

Having a grandchild makes you feel all warm and fuzzy inside.

As soon as we found out that our first daughter was with child, my wife came to me and asked me what I wanted to be called. She had already picked her name.

Nonnie.

There was no debate. It seemed like she'd had this name in her hope chest for most of her life.

I, on the other hand, had no idea what my grandfather name would be. I hadn't thought about it. I wasn't really in full-fledged grandfather mode at 54 years old. I needed to grow into the title, like the winter coats my mother bought me when I was young. She never bought coats that fit. Oh, heavens no. Since I might grow three inches before the next winter, she bought coats with the sleeves down past my wrists, halfway up my thumbs.

I remember the famous line of the saleslady, "Yes, that's a good size and he can grow into it."

In so doing, my mother wouldn't have to tum around and buy a new one before that winter season was even over. If I didn't have a monster growth spurt, I could even wear those extended-sleeve coats a third year. If not, she gave it to the next cousin in line.

Goodwill? Aw, hell naw.

God forbid we try to pull the old extended-sleeve trick on these spoiled, modern-day kids. No, not the kids who wear $200 Air Jordans.

No wonder Michael is worth $1.6 billion.

Now I really sound old.

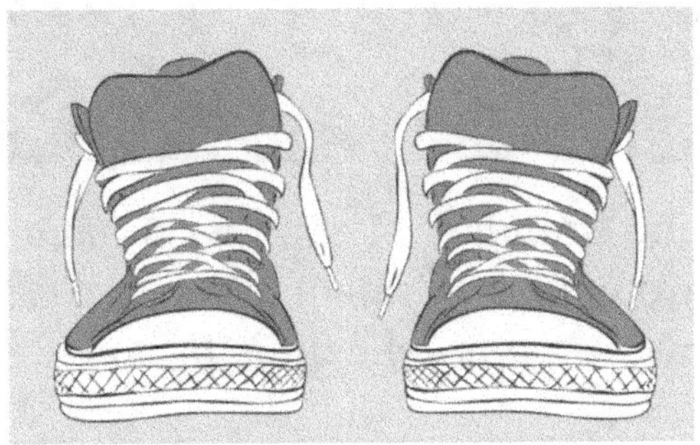

Moving on.

My youngest daughter, Kimberly, whom we never thought would even get married, was the first to tie the knot and the first to give us a grandson. She named him Noah.

I can still see her sitting up in her hospital bed with her glasses on, having had one of those easy deliveries that women so long for. Shortly after we passed the baby about and while still in the afterglow of the moment—what with the first nephew and first grandchild realization sinking in—I chose my grandfather name... Pap.

And the name change was on. Everybody took a step up.

To acquaintances, our given names stayed intact. We were still James, Jay, and Debbie, and Uncle James and Aunt Betty. But within our family, almost like magic, we converted like sinners to Christianity, all of us sliding up a notch, taking a life step up.

My father became Grandad. My mother became Gram. In fact, she absorbed two names—Gram and 2 G's. 2 G's was after her mother, Grammy... a name, she thought, too sacred to infringe upon.

I never complained; it was all part of the program. I had no choice.

But I have always wondered. What if I had refused to pick a grandfather name and, under fierce, family peer pressure, refused to buckle? Would my family have gotten together and picked a name for me? Probably not. I bet they would have called for an intervention.

They would have pleaded and then shockingly acquiesced: "No, that's okay, Daddy doesn't want to pick a name. I guess he doesn't want to be a grandfather. He thinks that will make him look old. That's his choice. Maybe the baby can call him James or Jim or Jimbo."

They all would mumble as they left: "What's up with him? Can't he play along? Asshole... dick... butthead..."

"Hey," I say. "I heard that."

There was no official agreement to move up to another call name. No trip to a judge or magistrate. It was just an accepted procedure, automatically done.

The funny thing is, although we rally around these new titles in ceremonial fashion, not only can't a newborn hail you by your freshly minted grandfather or grandmother name yet, he or she won't be able to say mommy and daddy for at least six months.

This was 14 years ago when grandparents pretty much stuck to the tried-and-true grandparent names. Signatures like

Grandad, Grammy, Gram, and the aforementioned Nonnie were common titles, chosen strictly by the book.

But I had my limits in picking a title, places where I absolutely refused to go. I categorically rebuffed a step up to monikers like Meemaw and Peepaw or Mawmaw and Pawpaw. These senior citizen monikers screamed of "Let's put these two oldsters in a rocking chair, out to pasture; they're no longer relevant. Make way for the new generation."

Even worse were Gramms and Gramps or Grammie and Grampie. Just say no to the name Grampie.

Any elderly person with a handle like that would have to wear Hush Puppies, refuse to buy a hearing aid, and grow hair in their ears.

Younger family members might come out to events and start yelling, "Hi, Grammie and Grampie. Have you had a bowel movement today?"

And let's not even speak of Baba and Gigi—they're Ukrainian nicknames, but they still make me shiver.

Don't take the bait.

As my six-year-old grandson would say, "Are you kidding me right now?"

I'm good with becoming a grandfather but do I have to scream, "Hey look, I'm an old man"?

Some grandfolks try to put a new spin on an old theme. A good friend of ours, Janet, incorporated her name into her new grandma tag, answering to the name of Granny Jannie.

Cute.

Lester Holt of *NBC News* fame mentioned on a talk show that he moved into the ranks of grandfathership and took on the name, Grand Dude. I can hear it now. "Hey look, Billy, here comes Grand Dude."

A new, hip take on an old theme but, I'd have to say, I'm not feelin' it. Nice try, Lester, but I'm on to you. Don't avoid the inevitable—no end runs; no getting the defensive back to bite on the out and going deep. Deep down inside, you're a Grampie just like the rest of us.

My brother-in-law, Bo (real name Lloyd), now deceased, took on the grandfather name of Pap Bo. I always liked that one; it rolled off the tongue nicely, had a fine ring to it.

So, getting a grandchild is an honor, a gift, a thing of beauty. But let's face it, it signals a new era. Now he's 15 and just received a new bicycle he's quite enamored with, but we all know where that's headed. The family is already tuned-in, mulling over the inevitable likelihood that, in a year or so, he'll be trading in his bicycle and beloved hover board for a learner's permit.

My father, once deep in the throes of the 1965 civil rights movement, is already trying to school him on how to deal with police should he be stopped in a car alone or riding with a friend or acquaintance. In quiet moments, my father puts his fist down softly on the dining room table and says, "We gotta watch him with those police."

And it's true. I've seen young kids run from pulled-over cars, a bad idea with disastrous results. Even I know adults who, as calm comfortable passengers in the backseat, tend to have more comments to make than the driver. As the driver obliges the officer, tail between legs, someone in the backseat is arguing, "That light was not red. You just pulled us over because we're black."

Noah, however, will be receiving the right to command a 3,500-pound vehicle like a diploma from high school. The honor will not just be a landmark moment for the extended Robinson clan but will coincide with the year I turn 70. Out with the old guard, in with the new.

Others will follow—four more boys and one girl will receive the speech from my father for as long as he's around to give it. When he's no longer up for the job, I'll assume the reins as the next in line.

The 10-year-old granddaughter, Amaya, in fact, is already asking if she can drive my car. What child, six years from driving glory, asks such a question?

"You're ten," I tell her incredulously.

She just keeps asking.

But there's no doubt about it, the be wary of the police speech will put me further and further into full-fledged, old-age mode.

Eventually, my family will band together and come after my car keys. But, then again, I'm not sure if it will be necessary. As long as my wife is healthy, I'm fine with playing wingman at times.

I'm no Maverick or Goose in *Top Gun*. I don't feel the "need... for speed." But I don't want to lose my wheels altogether.

No, I'm not walking in Gracie's shoes just yet. No one is thinking about asking for my keys.

Pap is free. For now.

Just don't call me Grampie.

5 Death Happens to Us All but I Want a Mulligan

It's natural to think about death when you're nudging toward 70. I wrote about how death begins creeping through one's cranium in midlife in my last work of art but it's nothing like what happens at this age.

"Death," I said back then, "has become, at least for me, a much more relevant proposition."

Relevant? That is a nice way to put it. Well, at the latter stages of life, let's just say it smacks you with an open hand on one side of the face and then follows up with the back hand on the other.

"Thanks, I needed that."

Let's say it's staring you in the face most of the time. You see it every day when you look in the mirror. Maybe I know too much.

Consider: I have 911 on my speed dial.

*

Every time I get some heaviness in the chest or what I think might be shortness of breath, I have 911 at the ready. On mental alert. I start thinking, *Should I call 911?* Then I go through the litany of heart attack symptoms that I've read in articles on the internet and watched on those TV talk shows.

Usually, I come to the conclusion that I'm not suffering from a heart attack but, rather, from pesky migraine symptoms which often cause tightening throughout the arms and chest.

My migraine symptoms have changed over the years, seemingly taking on a life of their own. They began in fourth grade with the classic aura, then vomiting for eight hours or so, where I felt like I was going to see my intestines in the toilet bowl, then a severe headache.

Of course, I had no idea what was happening and none of the country folk in Wichita, Kansas, knew either. I told them that I saw spots in front of my eyes—which I now know are called auras... and they laughed.

No one had even heard of the word migraine. There were no magazines in Wichita in 1961 with articles proclaiming: *How To Get Your Husband Aroused*, and *Hey, 4th Grader, You May be Suffering from a Migraine.*

But, over the years, the migraines mellowed considerably. They slowly graduated into the mild—almost daily—symptoms that I get now which begin with a mild vertigo, followed by the spasms outlined above, then the lingering headache.

I can usually tough these out. Sometimes a couple of Ibuprofen will do the trick. But my kidney guy advises against NSAIDs—non-steroidal anti-inflammatory drugs. This mandate is unfortunate; taking a couple of Tylenol is like sucking down a pair of Sugar Babies.

But then, as old age began to take hold, things started changing. I began to get sick headaches that were born from Lucifer himself, headaches that seemed to be some kind of collective monster made up of the worst symptoms of every migraine I've ever known—aura and vomiting from my first bout in the flatlands of Wichita, a weird feeling of euphoria, and eight hours of vomiting, sleep, vomiting, sleep, then finally, okay, it's over.

And the newest wrinkle—disorientation and vertigo from the pits of hell. They remind me of the movie where the alien took on the personalities of all its victims, a potpourri of the poor souls it had taken hostage throughout the previous two hours.

My PCP labels them "atypical" migraines. Every time I go in for a wellness visit, he makes a point of asking, "You haven't gotten any…?" He makes a circular motion with his finger about his head as if indicating that someone in the room is crazy.

But I know the gesture. It's the sign for super vertigo, the dreaded *atypical*, the call-911-migraine.

I recently saw a picture of a 5" fossilized tooth from an extinct 20-million-year-old Megalodon shark in Essex, England, held next to a normal sized shark tooth.

Ladies and gentlemen, meet Megalo-migraine.

In mid-motion, I shake my head no to the doctor. It's our little game of name that ailment.

The monster Megalodon is the worst of all. Suddenly, I began to develop severe room-spinning vertigo, disorientation to the point where I can't walk, along with extreme bouts of vomiting. On one occasion, as I lay incapacitated on a gurney in a hospital hallway, my family got hungry and picked my pockets for food money. I was so out of it I don't remember.

But they laugh when they think about the incident. "What were we supposed to do? We hadn't eaten and you zoned out." I've always found that pretty tacky.

The first time the monster Megalodon occurred it was a bit of a mystery among a group of physicians. As they huddled around my bed, a hospital physician labeled it a neurological problem, perhaps an aneurism. My neurologist and my PCP had no doubts that it was Megalodon, yet a brain MRI (I always joke that they first had to find my brain and then clean it) found nothing.

Then there are the stroke-related symptoms that I'm sure all of the older generation are burdened with. When stroke-like symptoms come calling, I immediately squeeze an index finger on one hand with a tightened fist of the other. If I pass that test, I sometimes look in the mirror to see if one side of my face is drooping. Now I hear that your tongue can even be drooping on one side.

Screw you guys; I'm not running to the mirror and inspecting my tongue.

The elderly are also burdened with life-and-death concerns that go beyond health. Every time I pay a visit to the hospital for a procedure—a false alarm, one of those wicked megrims, or drooping tongue—I am asked if I have a living will. That, of course, means that I have to spell out, while I'm living, what I want done when I can't speak for myself. I consider it more of a damn-near-dead will.

On this document, I would indicate whether I'm a candidate for DNR (do not resuscitate) and my family would have to honor it. This way, my wife and daughters wouldn't be fighting over the plug. They would just look wistfully at one another and say, "This is the way Pap wanted it."

But if I could hear them, I'd be shouting in silence, "No, I changed my mind! Oh well."

I intend to live forever or die trying.
—Groucho Marx

I think that animals have been wired right by our maker. As a Jewish friend of my wife says, "They don't know for nothin'." Translation: ignorance is bliss. It's not in them to fear death.

They don't talk about it or wonder what happens if they see a bright light. Their concerns center around finding enough food for them and their young to survive. Their thought processes aren't sophisticated enough to wonder what's going to happen after they die. At least not until they're being chased by a lion hell bent on having them for dinner. Then their instincts kick in and they run like the dickens to stay alive. I believe they say something like: "Aw, shit, death is imminent." Or, more likely, "This son of a bitch is trying to hurt me. I'm going to run because this isn't going to end well."

When a wildebeest's intuitions kick in and they know that it's time to migrate, 1.5 million of them travel 500 miles for food and water. Two hundred thousand zebras also make the trip. But I doubt if they worry about whether they will make it back before returning. They know what their destiny is going to be. They don't fear death until they timidly dip a hoof into crocodile-infested water. Then it hits them: "Damn, I might have to die to pull this off. Who the hell set this shit up?"

If it were humans making the swim, there would be a cacophony of excuses at the river:

"No, after you. I just ate. I have to wait 30 minutes."

"No, thank you. I'm waiting for a friend."

"Oh, that's nice of you, but I just had my hair done."

"I don't believe in migration. I don't even know what I'm doing here."

"I like your swimsuit; mine makes me look fat."

"I can't swim..."

All were snatched mid-excuse by an alligator who leaped from the water.

Eventually, a Michael Phelps type jumps in with a tight pair of trunks, a swim cap, and showing off a six-pack. He spurs other great swimmers and athletic types to take the plunge.

Some make it. Some... don't.

As the migration continues, some try to backtrack but are swallowed up by determined swimmers coming the other way.

Yeah, I'm a fan of *National Geographic* and exciting documentaries made on this amazing adventure. The migrators know what's waiting for them at the river's edge and no one wants to be the first to go. But instinct wins out over fear. The animals are hesitant at first, but once one brave soul starts the plunge, the stampede gets underway, and the buffet begins.

Make no mistake, the crocodiles know what's coming. Hey, they have instincts, too. After years and years of being served wildebeest and zebra meat at a certain time of year, they get the message. Even reptile Crocodylidae doesn't need a calendar to hear the dinner bell.

And so ends the cycle.

Well, the wildebeest and zebra have had their annual brush with death—although they don't have the slightest idea why—they will go back to life as normal. But for an old ager like me, death is a constant reminder that we're not here forever.

The problem isn't that we have an expiration date, the problem is that we think too much. We're too smart for our own good.

Well, to you people who want to play games with age I say, "How about kissing my light-brown behind?"

There are those of us who have gotten the notion that death is a choice. Keep yourself in good shape, eat the right foods, exercise, take vitamins, stay away from tobacco, don't drink to excess, and the grim reaper will steer clear of you. All fine and dandy. But you're going to die anyway.

Sooner or later, death is going to be the death of us all.

We see death in terms of the living.

I've heard people my age say: "I've had a good life. I'm ready to go." I really admire this kind of thinking. By the time we get to our elderly years we should be ready.

The fear of death follows the fear of life.
A man who lives fully is
prepared to die at any time.
—Mark Twain

I've heard all of the Bible stories about Noah and the whale, and Daniel in the lion's den. Nice anecdotes. But they don't begin to touch the surface.

Then, there is the religious side of death. Religion has become an entirely different thing for me in my older years. Age 70 should be a time when, like John Denver, you have your bags all packed and you're ready to go. I should be putting all of my teachings to use at this age. I should be dotting my Christian I's and crossing my spiritual T's. Just as my 401k should have been gathering interest over my working years, my spiritual annuity should have been gathering interest for me up to old age. And it should be a bull market.

Just between you and me, I'm a little spooked about dying. Drifting into the abyss of old age now, I'd like to have some idea of what happens, where I'm going. No guesswork, give me the straight poop.

Take heaven and hell, for instance. As a preacher's kid, I've been hearing about heaven and hell since I was seven years old. But now, with the rubber primed to meet the proverbial road, I'm getting all philosophical and opiniated about the subject.

So, okay, here's my primer. From what I've been told all my life, it's all pretty much cut and dry. Heaven is up and hell is, well, down... somewhere. God kicked Lucifer out of heaven and into hell to rule there and basically torture the hell souls for all eternity.

Consider it a paid leave. You know, like when a cop is involved in a questionable shooting and they don't want to kick him or her off the force. They put them in salaried purgatory, in essence saying, "We'd rather you hadn't gone and done that, but consider yourself in time out until we can figure out what to do with you."

I've lived on this premise for most of my life, but at this late date, weighed down by decades of maturity and common sense, the doubts have begun to kick in.

I pray to the Lord in heaven. Heaven is up, a no brainer; it only makes sense. Limitless blue skies and stars above the dark clouds, lightning, drenching rain. When you fly, you go up. When you release a balloon, it floats upward.

But this whole issue of hell. Where is it? It's down? Down where? Down somewhere where it's dark and hot. Hot as hell, if you will. We know the people we want to go there. We say it all the time. *You can go to hell! I hope he burns in hell!* Hell hath no fury like a woman scorned.

So who goes where?

When I die, I hope to go to heaven,
wherever the hell that is.
—Ayn Rand

Who takes the elevator to the ground floor? I mean, for real. Well, since no one has bothered to give me specifics, I've had to create my own roster.

I figure since my roll call vision happens to be on a Thursday, it's poker night with flames and moaning all around and residents all about. Around the table sits a cacophony of evil. Adolph Hitler, the elder stateman of Hades, pulled from his post-war bunker, has been engulfed in flames since the end of

WWII. He throws down his hand and snarls in German that he has five aces.

Charles Manson breaks into laughter. "Hey, mein Fuhrer, you look a little hot under the collar. Adolph, you try that crap every game. Don't you know the war is over?"

"Ja, und du hast Frauen deine schmutzige arbeit machen."

"Yeah, I let women do my dirty work," Manson scoffed. "That's how you keep your hands clean. And, yeah, I understand German in this hot-ass place."

The Fuhrer goes into a rant and then grudgingly takes an ace off the table.

But his game is cut short; demons swoop in to snatch the ultimate tyrant up and take him for his hourly trip to the gas chamber where Jewish apparitions give him a taste of his own evil. Heinrich Himmler is whisked up shortly thereafter.

"When you kill six million people," Ted Bundy scoffs, "what's the big deal about cheating at cards?" He casts a glance at Jeffrey Epstein. "Hey newbie, want to try your luck?"

"No thanks, I'm terrible at cards," Epstein answers.

"Yeah, you're not so good with money, either."

"Low blow, Ted," Epstein groans.

"What are you looking at, Weinstein?" John Wayne Gacy chimes in.

"Nothing," Jeffrey Epstein says. "And that's Epstein, clown boy, and leave me out of this."

"You had no class, Jeffrey," Gacy mutters. "At least I wore a clown suit."

"Hey, Saddam," Manson says, "what happened to those 72 virgins? You're down here with the rest of us. I don't see any virgins. Death sucks, don't it?"

"Akhrus ayaha alkhinziru!"

Manson's mouth opens wide. "Shut up, you pig? That's not very nice, Saddam."

"You too, Osama. Prayers aren't gonna help you. Gettin' tossed out of that World Trade Center time and time again while it's fallin' all to pieces. Is that your fate? That's a bitch."

"Hey Jeff, time for dinner," Ted Bundy yells.

Jeffrey Dahmer sits alone staring at the faces of all his victims—tortured and devoured.

"They're hungry, Jeff. They want an arm and a leg. HA! Turnabout is fair play."

One thing I can tell you for sure. I'm not going to the Satan Land. Sounds definite, doesn't it? I've made my share of mistakes—I've sworn deceitfully, I've used the Lord's name in vain, I've told my share of lies, I've cheated, strayed, squandered, and, more than once, I've returned items of clothing to clothiers after I had worn them (secret—make sure you keep the tags on).

Sorry, Eddie Bauer, LL Bean, Land's End.

And from what I've heard, a lot of others will join me. I keep hearing about these near-death experiences, visions where people on the operating table see a bright light which they swear is a beacon from heaven. Some scientists disagree, saying that dopamine, endorphins, and too much caffeine are responsible for the bliss.

Party poopers.

But I can't discuss heaven and hell without bringing up the book and movie that changed religion more than the Catholic Pope. Yes, I'm talking about you, William Peter Blatty. I'm talking about you, William Friedkin. Centuries of religious history including the origins of Christianity, Salem Witch trials, the Crusades, and *Raiders of the Lost Ark*, all act as second-class citizens, golf caddies to tongue wagging, green vomit spitting, and cross defiled vaginas—shows you where our heads are.

Release *The Exorcist* to the public and suddenly we believe. There really are demons from hell possessing little girls.

I know because Linda Blair's head twisted all the way around and she vomited up green stuff into a priest's face. I never saw that in the Bible.

Sure, it's just a movie. But these movie people are damned good at what they do. I can hear the demons. I can see the green shit. I can get a good look at little Regan's face and, damn, she's effed up.

Listen, I have no idea what happens in the afterlife and neither does anyone else.

But at 70, I'm getting more and more curious every day.

Frankly, I'm just dying to know. (HA!)

I need a little more time to figure this out. What's it gonna be? An afterlife, a former life, a rebirth? Whatever it is, I need a mulligan—pick my ball up in the thick weeds and put it down somewhere where I can get off a good shot.

I'm a slow starter. I'm laid back. I'm quiet; ask anybody. I'll be more aggressive the next time through. I'll write more stories. I'll put my glasses back on my nose faster (see chapter 8).

Oh, who am I kidding? It's one and done. You do the best you can the first time through. No second chances. No up, no extras. May the best man win.

Can I get a witness?

Somebody say amen.

6 What Can You Do When You Find Out You're Getting Old? Not a Damn Thing

Let's just be honest, here. In the war between youth and age, young and old, life and death, one thing is for sure—Father Time wins every battle.

Although I do still care about my appearance, it just isn't as important as it used to be.

When I look in the mirror and I see an aging face staring back at me, a face that looked better a scant two years ago, I say, "Damn, I look old. But what the hell can I do about it?" The answer is strong and immediate.

Not a damn thing.

It's not like it happens overnight. Your face changes slowly over time; you just don't know it. But there is something akin to time-lapse photography. Look at pictures of yourself over the years and note the results. We make comments like, "Look how young I looked in that picture."

As the old Vaudeville routine goes: "Slowly I turn, step by step, inch by inch…"

Then for some reason, it's like the cover comes off to reveal a painting, and you see what time, that wicked sun, and age have done to a once young and vibrant visage.

Oh, don't fall for that Cindy Crawford, Christie Brinkley, can't-tell-them-from-20-years-ago nonsense. For every one of them you have 50 Brooke Shields. Have you seen Brooke lately?

We paid an accomplished photo hanger to hang all of our framed photos when we downsized into our current home four years ago. He did a magnificent job. There are pictures of me dating back to high school days, wedding days, with my kids in their younger years when I was a big muscular guy. I walk by these photos every day.

Pictures are nice. When you keep them in the drawer. I liked the way I looked back then. Biceps, triceps, and deltoid muscles bulged through my clothing. I could make my deltoids jump up and down to my favorite songs. My thighs fought off attempts from mortal trousers to hold the line.

But I'm old now and I don't look that way anymore. Not that I care.

Those days are gone. I'm not trying to impress anyone. I'm not going to bars to meet women. I'm not visiting online dating sites. Besides, what can I do about it?

Not a damn thing.

In middle age, my feet once spread out to a size 12-4E from a manageable 11-D like a new house sinks after a few years of settling.

No big deal. Unless, that is, your abode was put on a landfill or an Indian burial ground. So you might see a few barely noticeable cracks in the walls. But you don't have to buy new shoes for your house. What can you do when your house settles?

Not a damn thing.

Well, I didn't have to put Buster Browns on my foundation, but I was aghast when my foot ligaments began their final—I hope—process of spreading out.

"This is it," I could hear them say. "The last time. You won't have to buy any more shoes after this."

Lies and more lies.

Again, as with middle age, I had a shoe roster that was set. I had casual shoes, dress shoes, and winter boots all lined up for duty. The boots were primed and ready for snow and slush when called upon. Now these trusty boots are just setting there looking at me. Like a car that I can't drive when I have somewhere to go.

It was swift and sudden but our time together is over, guys. I'll find another home for you.

But this time, I really got screwed royally. My feet have jettisoned to a 14-4EEE. Although sometimes a 14-2EE will get the job done. But the brand of footwear to which I have become attached doesn't carry the sizes I need. I have to buy them online without trying them on.

So, I have to watch my son-in-law—a shoe freak—and my grandsons wear all of these stylish, cute Air Jordans around that I can just admire.

Their feet stay the same size for a while and then grow in length and width. That's what growing feet do.

If there are perks for older people, one is that your body parts, including your feet, remain within striking distance whether it be up or down. Granted, old people shrink a bit, they lose their hair, they get those weird mineral spots. But there should come a time when you can have faith in your wardrobe. Feet have no right to just change sizes overnight.

Old people should be spared growth spurts. I shouldn't be passing down shoes to friends and family like my grandchildren pass clothing down to their brothers' cousins. My feet shouldn't be changing sizes. I should be done with that. It's a perk of old age. I'm old. I should have perks.

So, like saying goodbye to good friends that I have met over the years, I bid a fond farewell to all the footwear of my middle years. Saying *adios* to a perfectly suitable pair of plimsolls is like being forced to get rid of comrades you still feel a fondness for or breaking up with a girlfriend whose company you still enjoy and whom you still find attractive.

"What did I do wrong?" these ladies would ask tearfully.

"I'm so sorry," would be the reply. "It's not you; it's me. We just don't... fit anymore."

Is there no justice in this world? And what can I do about it?

Not a damn thing.

Just a few days ago, a picture circulated within the family of my oldest daughter Jaime and me when she graduated from middle school. Aside from the fact that I was making one of my weird faces that made me look like a zombie, the first thing that caught my eye was my hair—it was jet black. Anyone who knows me now knows that my hair is full of gray.

Oh sure, I could color it. I could make my locks look like they did some 30 years ago. But why bother? It is, as they say, what it is. Coloring your hair puts out a false statement to the world. It says, "I'm flipping that hourglass. I'm trying to turn back the hours of time." It's called futility. And what can I do about futility?

Not a damn thing.

It's not unusual—as singer Tom Jones would say—to see men my age with their belly hanging over their belt—some more than others. I often use these individuals as examples—bellwethers as it were—when it comes to my own protruding abdomen.

What can I do about it?

Actually, there is something.

I can say, "No matter how old I get, I'll be damned if I ever look like that."

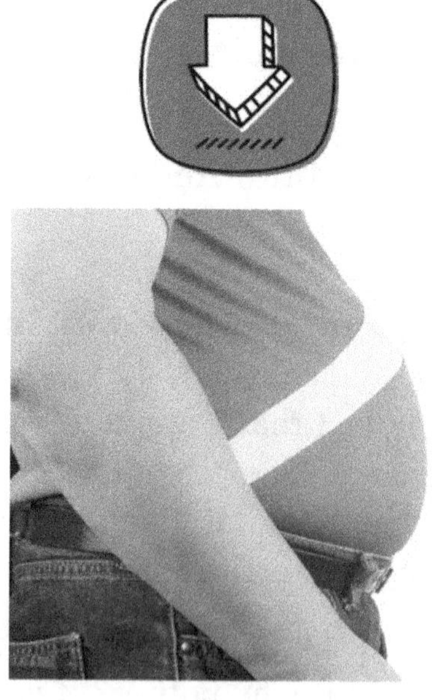

There are limits to what old age and the "not a damn thing," mantra can do. If you're a guy and you look into a mirror and see some semblance of the above picture, Google Weight Watchers.

Cause, dude, you're fat.

Getting up in years doesn't excuse you from keeping things under some modicum of control. This bloke doesn't even look that old. He needs to lighten up on the carbs. Imagine what he'll look like when he's my age. This gentleman deserves the Poppin' Fresh poke. And by rules of the Old-Age Geneva Convention, he is not permitted to return said poke.

See the next chapter for an explanation of the above reference.

Don't let old age and its friends futility and disgust take you totally over the edge. It's true, there are some things we have no control over, but other things we can. Can we control our attitudes? Can we keep a healthy outlook and do the things we enjoy doing as best we can?

You're damn right, we can.

Can we stay as close to close friends and family as possible—laugh, play games, read, enjoy life?

You're damn right, we can.

Sure, I just bought a pair of $200 great-looking Hoka shoes online that I really liked but that, deep down, knew weren't going to fit.

Can I wave a magic wand over these shoes and make them fit?

No, and it really ticks me off. All I want is a pair of shoes that fit my feet!

The search goes on.

7 Pop'n Fresh, You Magnificent Bastard: a Stylish Interlude

Okay, I admit it. This title isn't really accurate. At least not as far as my true feelings go. I hearken back to the days of the ridiculously cute, adorable, Pillsbury Dough Boy mascot, Pop'n Fresh. You know, the chubby little doughboy in the baker's outfit—the chef's hat and scarf, that gave out this little giggle when poked in the tummy by someone from out of the shot.

Well, I didn't find His Freshness to be magnificent at all, but rather, I expressed the desire to pop Mr. Fresh in the oven until he looked like Buckwheat from *The Little Rascals*.

But on with my old-age interlude.

About a year ago, around the time when my eye problems were beginning, I was sitting at our dining room table in the home my wife and I share with my parents. In attendance were my mother, my aunt (her sister), and my two cousins who are brother and sister.

The reason for our get together was Albie, one of the two cousins at the table, was visiting from Maryland.

Albie and I go way back. When I was but a sophomore in college—1971, Roberto Clemente died in his tragic plane crash that year while we were on our trip—Albert was but a wee lad of 14, and we began making summer treks to his sister's (my cousin's) home in Portsmouth, Rhode Island. Having met my future wife at age 22, he and I ventured off to Portsmouth and I came back with a handmade leather lady's purse for the young woman who was destined to become my fiancée in 1974.

When I got married two years later, Albert would be my best man. And so the relationship continued through babies and grandchildren, early parent deaths and suicides.

Now as we sat about the table and shot the proverbial bull, the subject came around to my troublesome eyes that were just starting to give me problems post cataract surgery.

I was in with the crowd, minding my own business, listening to the chatter.

My eye problems were not really something I wanted to discuss. But the inquisition began.

"Where did you have your eye surgery done?" someone chirped.

I reluctantly told them the name of the company despite the fact that I knew no one would recognize the name and that it was senseless to say it.

"What's the doctor's name?" someone else asked.

Although, I became familiar with a few, there were numerous technicians and eye surgeons in the office and I was never sure which one I was going to get from one visit to the next.

"There are a lot of doctors," I said, becoming annoyed. "I don't always see the same one." *And you wouldn't know him if I told you,* I thought. *So let's end this line of questioning and get out of my business.*

Times had changed. We used to be close, and sit around and joke about the good times. Now it was me being grilled by eighty and ninety-year-olds.

The interrogation continued.

My aunt picked up the questioning. "I thought we decided that you were going to go to another doctor and get a second opinion?"

The doctor that we had discussed in private was actually an optician and I had second thoughts about seeing an optician who would probably not be able to shed any more light on the situation. After all, even though an optometrist can detect a lot in an exam, bottom line, I wasn't in the market for glasses.

"I decided not to do that," I said. "She couldn't tell me any more than the doctors could."

My mother then gave me some tough love. "We're just trying to help you," she said. "Why are you being such an asshole?"

It took a while to sink in, but it suddenly hit me that my mother had just called me an asshole. This act was definitely a product of age and, let's call it, eccentricity.

Consider that, when I was younger, she would never would have greeted me in the morning with a hale and hearty, "Get up, asshole."

Allow me to say that we're anything but the Cleavers. My mother calls me a shitass quite often. Despite the fact that it's a guttural term, we're a down-to-earth family. Within our circle, it's a harmless, playful type term that my grandmother called my grandfather when he got on her nerves, the worst thing she ever called him.

Unfortunately, every time my mother calls me that, she also plies me with the story.

"Boy, if Grammy called Papa that, she was really mad at him. He would turn his back and laugh, and his shoulders would shake. Then she would really get mad."

It must have been the hundredth time she had passed that story along but I'm sure it only seems that way. In reality, it's only, oh, I don't know, 49 or 50.

"Really," I say. "I didn't know that." I don't know if she fields the sarcasm.

I breathe a breath of here we go again. *Woo-saw. Don't scream, I think. She's my mother. She's 92.* But I always wonder, is it senility, or is she just showing off?

At any rate, being called an asshole has definitely raised the ante a bit.

I looked at my cousin, Albie whose expression said, *I don't believe she said that. Shitass would have been okay but...*

Everything was a blur after that.

Albie talked about Papa and how our grandfather challenged him with vocabulary words. I was pretty disgusted by this time. *Who the "f" cares*, I thought?

Albie's mother, Vonda, my mother's sister, as I spoke of previously, actually lived with us on the third floor of the famous 1400 Pennsylvania mansion and, in the end, I carried her down two flights of stairs when she was dying of cancer.

She died two days later.

I could barely haul my own arse down all of those steps now without maintaining a steady grip on the banister.

Despite our history, I never got to speak with Albie one-on-one that evening. As we rose from the table, he gave me one of those Pop'n Fresh pokes to the stomach.

I didn't giggle.

I hate it when someone defiles my abdomen. How rude. I'm tempted to give them a Moe to Curly, Three Stooges, two-finger poke in the eyes. It's unlikely that they will know how to block the poke defensively.

What a shock that would be—the poor recipient of the poke screaming, bent over in pain, hands covering the eyes, wondering if their eyesight is still intact. Poor devils. But I would be insolent, leaning over them in defiance.

Poke my tummy now, bitch!

I had no idea what he was thinking. Stomach pokes mean a lot of things. Usually they mean, *What's that big thing you got growing there, champ?* My cousin's jab could have said: "I haven't seen you in a long time. You're getting a little rowdy around the middle there, aren't you? It comes with the territory. Sorry I didn't get to speak with you on this trip. Say hello to Debbie."

Too bad we never got some alone time, but the ravages of old age somehow got in the way. Relatives get old. They lose touch. They sometimes get caught up in the small, trivial stuff, forgetting the good things. They stutter on meaningless jargon like the names of my ophthalmologists.

Hey, remember Moses? It hasn't been 40 years but let me go.

Sometimes, coming together in confluence from different worlds, having not communicated for some time, doesn't make for a whole lot to say.

I'm a veteran of those Discovery + shows like *Evil Lives Here*, *American Monster*, and *See No Evil*—a drama where murders and abductions are solved using surveillance cameras placed on businesses such as Sheetz convenience stores, Walmart, gyms, restaurants, night clubs and even private homes.

Sure, these shows be a little gruesome but isn't life a little gruesome at times?

I remember a show where a family was devastated to learn that one of their own was a serial killer—raping and murdering women for years without their knowing.

After police detectives caught their murdering son and brother, after watching hour upon hour of surveillance footage as well as intense investigation, he was convicted and sent to jail for life without parole.

Despite the heinous nature of his crimes, the killer's brother visited him in jail but, after a while, stopped the visits because he said that his brother had been in jail so long that his growth as an individual ceased due to his imprisonment and lack of social interaction.

He felt they had nothing to talk about.

But I think that he could have at least been a lifeline for his brother, kept him informed on what was going on in the world and with the family but, hey, given the circumstances, maybe the brother didn't deserve it.

Maybe being isolated was his penalty.

Small talk ruled the rest of our evening at our dining room table. Like the prisoner—minus the rape, murder and other nefarious behavior—we were limited in what we had to say.

No one else called me an asshole for the rest of the evening. And that was a good thing.

I longed for the days when we were younger, more vibrant, more in touch with society, and more in touch with ourselves.

But that's not going to happen. Old age has seen to that.

8 Pop'n Fresh Part II
Hey, I Really Like That Cane

On August 22nd of 2021, a family reunion was held in a local Pittsburgh Park known as North Park. August 22nd is noteworthy because I was born on this day almost 70 years ago.

The get together was uneventful—which was good—and was attended by some of my favorite relatives. The affair was laid back and humble with no crazy uncle there who might act a fool or whom you might worry about around the younger children.

Hey, a lot of families have an uncle like that.

No one organized any of those picnic games—no potato sack races; no softball games; in other words, nothing that requires any hand-eye coordination or physical strength of any kind. The big reason for this lack of activity was the crippling effects of age and older age, and the fact that most of us were steaming toward the geriatric community.

I remember when my father directed a Presbyterian Camp back in the early '60s. I was about 10 years old and having to participate in the most infantile camp games ever.

For instance, rather than a tried-and-true, potato-sack race, entrants got on their hands and knees and pushed an actual potato with their nose for a pre-determined distance to the finish line.

The race started. Amazingly, I was winning but my glasses slipped off my nose about halfway through and by the time I made adjustments, I lost valuable time and unfortunately, the race. I lost the event by a nose (HA!).

There was much commentary from the crowd after the event. Included were Rev. and Mrs. Robinson. From what I gathered, the sentiment concerning the big potato-nose race went like this: "He was winning and all he had to do was stop to quickly put his glasses on his nose but instead of pushing them up quickly he went like this"…

Someone in the group made a gesture with the index finger pushing the glasses up the bridge of the nose in super slow motion.

(Laughter)

I recently had an epiphany—how about suggesting to a ten-year-old kid that he take his glasses off before taking part in a spud-on-muzzle match!

All in keeping with my mantra of the slowest kid in the world.

My counselor's parting words to my father were kind but he also said: "He's such a nice kid but he's so s-l-o-o-o-w!

So, with no such gamesmanship at our picnic, no organized strife, we oldsters were able to sit around, eat and talk—more eating than talking.

Later, as I sat in my office writing, the doorbell rang and I heard voices. My mother yelled for me to come downstairs. As I got myself together to make the trip, my mother called for me again but this time it wasn't a yell, it was more like a scream.

My anger began to surface; I could tell she was showing off.

As I got halfway down the steps, I couldn't wait to say, "I heard you the first time." But she didn't hear me; she was too busy talking to my cousin's grandchild explaining why she could shriek for me at 110 decibels with no worry of reprisal.

"...cause I can beat his butt," I heard her saying to the girl in her own animated way.

One notch away from the seventy-mile marker, I thought, *and I'm still getting threatened with butt whippings.* The funny thing is, I don't ever think I got a for-real spanking when I was growing up. I was too much of a wimp.

But right at this time, I heard a large group of my relatives from the picnic break into a rendition of *Happy Birthday.* Not one of my favorite songs but a really nice gesture. They had no doubt gone to dinner and made it a point to stop by and honor the fact that I'd managed to keep breathing for another year.

I thanked everyone and then headed straight for my cousin Buddy—a man five years my senior and, himself, endowed with quite a few ailments—who was leaning on a very unique cane—a fancy walking stick of the solid-wood variety.

Talk about how old age sucks. With everything going on in the world including Covid-19 and its variants, I actually engaged him in a fascinating conversation about a walking stick. Really?

My knees had 15,000 miles of tread left, as you may recall, and have received several cortisone shots in the past few years. They have been feeling better and I had begun to forgo the steroids.

But that hip issue that I talked about before... my hip had really gotten ornery. After a precipitous dip in the weather, my right hip began to do its best impression of Dr. Jekyll and Mr. Hyde. Dr. Jekyll would accompany me for a few steps and then Mr. Hyde would interrupt.

It went like this: Step, step, step... yo, dude, Mr. Hyde is here. Ah!

I never know when the hip is about to give out, therefore a cane is standard equipment.

I was supposed to have it x-rayed by my orthopedist, but I bailed on him. I knew the photo would be ugly and I envisioned another left eye displacement experience.

"Uh, oh," he would say after a look at the x-rays. "That hip has to come out. Let me see if I can get you on today's schedule."

When he returned, the exam room would be empty and the receptionist would ask who the man was that ran down the hall to the elevators.

"On the way he screamed something about damn you, Dr. Hyde."

I took a guess and asked my cousin if he got the cane on Amazon and doggone if I wasn't right. He told me that he ordered a 36" but he wished he had gotten a 37". I told him that I would order a 37".

Wow, cane talk can be so fascinating.

Wondering what size cane I should order? What with our democracy under attack? What with plain-old people walking around shooting into crowds with AK47s? You've got to be kidding me.

After all of the guests left, I headed to my computer, pulled up Amazon and went straight for the walking canes. I found one with a lion's head that I really liked but choked on the cost: $100.00.

One hundred bucks for a cane? Really?

It looked like the one with the silver handle that Lon Chaney used to kill the werewolf in the original 1941 movie, *The Wolfman.* Only the one I had my eye on had a gold handle.

In case you're not familiar with the classic *Wolfman*, Lon Chaney was bitten in his encounter with the werewolf, of course, and developed serious consequences when the moon was full. A gypsy woman delivered the bad news, "Whoever is bitten by a werewolf and lives becomes a werewolf himself. Have you been bitten?"

"Yes."

"Have a nice day."

I'll just limp.

I decided against such an expensive walking device at this point in my life because my pain was sporadic. I could walk without assistance probably 90% of the time. Still, I saved it in my cart.

I mingled with my guests for a while but after a long day of picnicking they quickly fled the scene. Birthday number 69 was in the books.

Sixty-nine, as in the eight-day Jewish holiday Passover—69 passed over for the landmark 70.

I'll have my cane by then. Beware the full moon.

9 These Eyes: Part II
Oh, and About That Little Cancer Thing

It's not bad enough that many of the typical culprits go awry during the later years—feet, knees, hips, *feet*, eyes—but then ailments piggyback other ailments.

Cue The Guess Who.

After the, *so you actually thought you were going to get real laser surgery* in 2019 for my cataracts, problems began to surface, at first, I was delighted. My vision had improved dramatically, and I could see without glasses or contact lenses for the first time since grade school. I bought the readers that I knew I would need according to the no-sunroof, no-leather contract I signed.

But I continued to have problems with blurry vision and was given steroid drops (prednisolone acetate) for what they call "rebound" inflammation in both eyes for an extended period of time.

Hence the conversation at the dining-room table of my extended eye problems, followed by the concluding of worshipping at the feet of Pop'n Fresh.

Eventually, the drops—weak little things that they were—became ineffective against the evil. That's when, during one visit, a doctor decided that a shot in the eye... yes, a needle injected into my orb... with a stronger steroid would do it.

And, by golly, it did.

And just so we could even things out, when I got the same problem in the other eye, and was presented with the needle option again I said, "Oh, what the heck, what's say we stick a needle in that one, too? That will fix it."

And, gosh darn it, it did. But not for long.

Consider these little pricks a bandage, that finger you put in the dam of life.

I should have seen it coming.

John, Paul, George, and Ringo... I should have known better.

I should have known that this eye issue was going to be an ongoing thing. I should have known that I'd had a long run of good weather through my younger and middle life and that storm clouds were rolling in to welcome me to old-man hood.

After all, that's what storm clouds do. After an extended high-pressure system (I've been listening to meteorologist lingo for years, now it's time to show my skills) provides sunny dry weather for a week, a cold front always comes in from the south or the north with a ton of clouds and rain or snow and basically turns everything to shit.

Will this friggin' rain ever stop?

Go find the Biblical Noah and get him to work on the ark. Then flip houses, and see how many animals he can round up.

There could be issues.

The humane people aren't going to allow bears and tigers and elephants to be herded onto a big boat. Look what they did to the circus. Barnum and Bailey would be reduced to clowns, poodles, and motorcycles in a cage.

As I got through my initial problems, my eyes upped the ante. In August of 2020, as I sat innocently at my computer, I began to see a swirling group of "floaters" in my right eye that I described to the doctors like a tornado similar to the one that knocked Dorothy unconscious before her trip to Oz.

I would discover that my little tornado was caused by a displaced retina as well as several retinal tears.

Not good.

Surgery was performed immediately by a retinal and vitreoretinal surgeon. As I lie on the gurney waiting for my procedure, wearing one of those weird bonnets, I wasn't as nervous as much about the process as by the recovery regimen this skilled surgeon prepared me for.

He walked me through my recuperation by saying that I would have to sleep on my left side, and during waking hours, lie on my left side for 45 minutes of every hour. During those 15 minutes that I was permitted to walk about, I must keep my head down, face to the floor.

I envisioned Groucho Marx minus the cigar.

A hydrogen bubble was placed on the retina which would float to the area of the displacement and stabilize the region.

A bubble?

I was delighted that a cute little bubble was on the job. Hawaiian singer Don Ho wrote a song entitled *Tiny Bubbles*, Lawrence Welk began his show with a champagne pop and bubbles floating about, and babies blow bubbles to the delight of their parents—but this gas bubble wasn't cute.

This bubble was a medical necessity, a necessary evil, a gassy effervescence that would aid the healing process.

But it makes life miserable.

When I looked down to eat, I was looking through the bubble. The food tasted the same but, viewed through hydrogen gas, was less appealing.

Also, the bubble was in my right eye but, somehow, it bullied the left eye into submission and obstructed my entire line of sight.

Bottom line, when one eye is in such peril, it makes you think. You realize how fragile your sight is. How with one eye gone, you develop some empathy with Sammy Davis, Jr., feeling as if you're just one step away from Ray Charles.

Wouldn't you know I would see a documentary on Frank Sinatra on Netflix in which it was described how Sammy Davis, Jr., lost his eye? It appeared that during an automobile accident, his eye hit the huge middle of those old steering wheels and just popped out.

I obeyed my instructions post procedure and all went well. Okay, so, at times, I stayed up a bit longer than 15 minutes, but I found creative ways to do the Groucho Marx. You have to look down if you have a laptop, right? And you have to look down to play piano keys even if you're a not-so-good pianist.

Even though I cheated the system, my retina healed and my right eye returned to normal.

Fortunately, Dorothy's tornado never appeared in my eye again. But on May 25, 2021, a tear in the left eye was found which was repaired by a short laser procedure, an actual, for-real laser procedure.

The next day, I returned to the hospital to see one of the eye doctors for, what I expected to be a quick, everything looks good visit, but the doctor looked into my eye, rolled his chair back, and said... "Um."

An eye doctor saying, "um," reminds me of an old Bill Cosby album where he jokes that the last thing you want to hear a surgeon say during an operation is, "Oops."

As it turns out, my small tear had gone berserk, apparently invited 10 of its buddies to the party and, for good measure, another retinal tear had also come along to join the fun.

"Um..."

Bad enough.

But while I was dealing with this second ocular emergency, another issue rudely interrupted. My left eye concerns had bullied their way past an appointment already scheduled for the following day. It had rear-ended an urgent situation waiting for take-off, crashing my May 27th cancer party.

I told the doctor that I had a cancer procedure, called a Space OAR, the following day that I had prepared for all week. Undaunted, he told me in no uncertain terms, "This takes priority over that."

Sight trumps cancer? Apparently so, when the cancer is of the highly curable, prostate variety and not urgent. It wasn't like I was going in for some kind of life-saving tumor removal. The procedure could be rescheduled.

So how did I find out about the cancer, anyway?

Well, in the nine months between the right eye debacle and the left eye tears and detachment, my PSA number was slowly climbing. PSA, of course, stands for prostate-specific-antigen—an indicator of prostate health in men.

My PCP routinely ordered a blood test to check my PSA every year. My PSA numbers had been hanging around 3.5, half a click below the magic cut-off number of 4.0, for several years.

But before I go any further, allow me to introduce you to my nemesis, MyChart.

MyChart is one of those services provided by a healthcare company—an internet website that delivers subscribers the ability to pay bills, leave messages for their physicians, cancel and book appointments, and most importantly, check test results and pathology reports.

Courtesy of MyChart, I kept track of my PSA numbers until, at the age of 67, they began to rise. Twelve months after my wellness check, I paid a call to a lab for blood tests, visited MyChart the next day for results—he's a fast little devil—held my breath and discovered that I had shot past the landmark 4.0 cut-off. My PSA had jumped to 4.7.

I snarled, "Shit!" with great gusto through clenched teeth.

I expected my PCP to ship me to a urologist without haste but I dodged a bullet. He decided that we should keep an eye on the number and wait. When my next visit rolled around, I was sure that my numbers had leveled off. After the blood test, I paid a visit to my adversary MyChart for a ruling.

I took a deep breath and peeked. The numbers don't lie—5.7.

I uttered the same foul invective through clenched teeth, then saw it and raised it a "Son of a bitch!" Then concern stepped in.

The gig was up.

I made a trip to the urologist, and he gave me a choice: take one of those wait-and-see approaches or bite the bullet and undergo a needle biopsy—a procedure where pieces of the prostate are snipped and biopsied.

I donned my big-boy pants. I chose the biopsy.

I knew of the test but didn't realize it was one of the most unpleasant techniques ever concocted. It took two to three weeks to recover.

After the event, the doctor told my wife that he had taken 25 snips from the prostate to be sure but didn't expect anything to come out of it. "Oh, and by the way," he mentioned in passing, "his bowels moved during the procedure."

My daughter, the nurse, says it happens often in surgery. They even have a name for it—code brown.

I was informed to wait a week and a half for results.

Enter MyChart. I covered my eyes and looked through my fingers as if about to watch a horror movie. I was.

The results read as follows:

1. Prostate, Left apex, Ultrasound-Guided Needle Biopsy
   a. Invasive (Sounded like something from a Sigourney Weaver, *Alien* movie) Prostatic Adenocarcenoma Involving approximately 40% of submitted tissue

Now, I'm no doctor but there were two words that concerned me there. *Invasive* means it's not supposed to be there, and *carcinoma* is, well, cancer.

No swearing, no concern this go-round. Just shock. I was tearing up when I heard my son-in-law's voice as he ventured up the steps. That did it. I grabbed a tissue and began sobbing uncontrollable. Something about that "C" word just rubs you the wrong way.

After a minute or so, my voice of reason showed up. And it wasn't mincing words.

"Damn, dude," it said. "You're crying like a little bitch. Get a hold of yourself. You're darn near 70 years old. Children get cancer. Haven't you seen the commercials? They've obviously had several bouts of chemotherapy and lost their hair. Things will work out. And, by the way, you have company."

"Thanks," I sniffed, "I needed that."

My son-in-law just stood there, not knowing whether to console me or just let me weep in solitude. He chose the silent approach.

It was a crisis sandwich—two old-age-related eye issues with a bout of cancer in between. Hold the onions. Each battling for supremacy.

The eyes would have it. But this I know; I will undergo two bouts of radiation for two and a half weeks with a 90% cure rate for this type of cancer. As people often say, "If you're going to get cancer, prostate cancer is the one to get."

Oh, thank God for that.

A bit of left-handed positivity wrapped around a generous helping of gloom and doom if ever I've heard it.

But I'll take whatever I can get.

MyChart, damn you anyhow.

10 How Do You Know When You're Getting Old?

YOU KNOW YOU'RE GETTING OLD WHEN:

You carry a jacket into the restaurant or movie.

I've never really noticed older people carrying sweaters and light jackets into restaurants and movies prior to this. Why do they do that? Obviously, because these establishments tend to go overboard with the air conditioning.

At this age, I've noticed that I tend to think, Boy, a jacket or even one of my light sweatshirts that I left at home would sure feel good right now. I imagine the garment hanging in the closet doing me no good, in fact, laughing at me.

What the hell's so funny?

I've never had these thoughts before. Why does one get cold in a chilly restaurant when they get older? Does this make me a wuss? No, it's a matter of well-being. I swap pride for comfort. I'd much rather be warm than masculine. It's all part of the maturity that comes from growing old.

That coupled with the fact that I just don't give a damn.

So what do you do? Well, as wussy as it seems, you carry a jacket around in the car. As you depart your domicile, your wife asks, "Do you have your jacket? I saw it in the house somewhere."

Certainly, you don't ask the other patrons about the trend; you don't have to. You see them toting their sweaters and jackets into the eatery also.

YOU KNOW YOU'RE GETTING OLD WHEN:

You realize you can't run anymore.

Yeah, that's right. I can't run anymore. I was coming from my daughter's house, which is about 50 yards behind ours. Our garages face one another so it's not like I had to search for my keys to get in the door. Unfortunately, it was raining. I attempted a quick jaunt to keep from getting soaked but I couldn't even manage a trot. With my foot aching from planter fasciitis, my knees on hiatus, and my right hip on loan from my orthopedist for replacement, I had no choice but to get wet.

Is that what I'm reduced to? Getting soaked in a storm because I can't quicken my gait?

Man, that sucks.

This might sound farfetched but what if I were, God forbid, being chased by Freddy Kruger or worse, Jason from Friday the 13th?

Perhaps the adrenaline coursing through my body would summon the energy to run for my life. Funny, it doesn't help any of those young girls who are massacred in the myriad of slasher movies. Jamie Lee Curtis is the only one who managed to go unscathed.

Worse, what if I'd had a cane? Wait, the thought of that is going to send me into hysterics. Swinging my cane at Jason Vorhees, Jason might break down with laughter, allowing me to escape.

Enough. Moving on.

You may find this theory ridiculous but I'm the one who would be sliced and diced. Carrying a firearm wouldn't help. You know the bastard won't die.

You get the point. I'll leave it at that.

YOU KNOW YOU'RE GETTING OLD WHEN:

You get an email from your high-school reunion committee asking if you will attend your 50th class reunion.

Are you kidding me right now? Fifty years?

I knew the fifty-year reunion was coming I just hadn't seen it in writing. I had gotten a preliminary heads-up email from one of my classmates a year earlier who had been tasked with the job of collecting addresses of graduates. Her email was both informative and depressive.

After telling me that she was shocked that I was still in, "the 'Burgh," she began rattling off names of classmates who wouldn't be able to make it to the reunion due to a major handicap: death.

The fact that they were no longer with us hit me pretty hard.

I knew them all and considered them friends.

I began to wonder how they died and when.

You see, way back in 1965, a curriculum was created in the Pittsburgh School System known as the Scholar's Program. Based on achievement test scores and teacher recommendations, students skipped their final year of middle school and were jettisoned into high school in eighth grade.

I thought back and wondered if I had been a bit too immature for such a leap. In terms of English Literature, I jumped from seventh grade and landed right into Nathaniel Hawthorne's lap in high school, having to get a grip on his famed House of Seven Gables novel.

When I got older, I took a peek at Mr. Hawthorne's classic just to see if my mature mind could handle it.

It made even less sense than it did when I was 13.

YOU KNOW YOU'RE GETTING OLD WHEN:

You begin to realize that all of the rigamarole, rules, and theories that circulated around throughout your life about cars are blown a bit out of proportion.

For instance, you begin to think about people who say, "I just want basic transportation, something to get me from point A to point B."

Isn't that the whole point?

Are they trying to prove how frugal they are or blow smoke up your rear rather than admit they can't afford a decent car? Either way, I don't care. And cars lose half of their value the minute you drive them off the lot.

Accountants take the fun out of everything. They'll tell you to keep a car for 10 to 15 years. I know a lot of marriages that didn't last that long.

I've had friends and family who aspire to the accountant philosophy, who throughout my younger days gave me shade and little verbal shots because I traded in a car faster that they thought I should have (oh, my God) ...

before it was paid for, before I had equity even, before every payment in the book had been made. There are rules, regulations, and adult responsibilities that come with owning a car.

You just don't do that. Furthermore, their accountant says you shouldn't do that.

I'm frivolous, I'm irresponsible; I traded in my car six years too soon. Imagine the money I lost. All I really needed was something to get me from point A to point B. I could have opened a Roth IRA or put $5,000 in the bank. I repeat...

Oh... my... God...

My problem was... I liked cars. Still do.

When those damned automakers kept coming out with flashy models with all of the latest equipment my heart started to skip a beat and my mind began to race.

When those Car and Driver and Road and Track magazines landed in the mailbox every month, I salivated. I got Playboy magazines in the same mailbox that didn't have the same effect.

When it came to Playboy, I figured after you've seen two, you've pretty much seen them all.

No, I said to myself. Come on, pay off this car. Keep it another five years. Open a Roth IRA with that car payment (whatever that is). Be practical.

However, now I have to ask myself, are automobiles really that important in the scheme of things? Are they worth that type of scrutiny and consternation? Should we judge people by the cars they drive?

And another thing. At my stage of life, I hear people—usually in the final decade of their lifetimes—say, "This will probably be my last car."

Really? Do you want to sound the death knell with an automobile? Do you really want to align your life expectancy to 4,000 pounds of metal, plastic, leather, rubber, and glass?

I have a better idea. Take things as they come. Don't look too far into the future when you don't know how much future you have. You might want to sneak another car in on the grim reaper. Buy the insurance (if they offer insurance). Bequeath the car to your spouse, a child or grandchild, or Goodwill.

When it comes down to it, we take cars too seriously.

I remember when I was working at U.S. Steel in 1982 (wow, has it been that long?) and talking to a co-worker while working an all-night study at one of the mills. Somehow, we got on the subject of cars and he told me that his brother-in-law worked at the car auction and that whenever he wanted a car, he just told his brother-in-law what he wanted.

To be more specific, he just pointed him in the right direction by saying, "I want a big car," or "I want a medium size car," and the brother-in-law would do the rest. So much for test drives, price haggling, and having to wait while the salesman supposedly discusses your deal with his manager.

Hey, come to think of it, maybe my co-worker was ahead of his time. This guy obviously wasn't into cars. I can imagine what he said when he "took delivery" of the vehicle.

"Hey, that's a good-looking car. What is it?"

But car lover that I was, I was a bit shocked. He doesn't even pick his own car? Heresy, I thought.

Times have changed. I figure, life is too short for pussyfooting around with car rules and guidelines. Pick a car and do whatever the hell you want with it.

If I subscribe to the keep your car 10-15 years concept, my life may be over and out by the time the parameter ends.

When you're my age, I say, "Wear your coat, sweater or fleece to the movie or restaurant like a badge of honor. If you can't run, then skip or walk as quickly as possible, or hop if chased by Jason Vorhees from Friday the 13th."

If all else fails, stand your ground and dazzle him with magic tricks.

If you get an invitation to a class reunion that's 40 years or higher, just be glad you're not on that didn't-make-it list.

And finally, do whatever you want with your automobile. In the end, it means nothing.

11 Age Is Just a Number Except When It Comes to Age 70

When my oldest daughter—now 42—reached a birthday in her younger days (say age four or five), she always tried to make herself a little older. Not satisfied with her current year, she tried to push the envelope. For instance, with her fifth year approaching, she would jump the gun and announce, "Next year I'll be six."

We all got a kick out of it. We still do.

Not surprisingly, she eventually lost the desire to advance her age. What woman wouldn't? After all, for a woman to advance her age another year is not just crazy, it's institution worthy.

An old ager like me, I seem to be falling into the same trap. But for different reasons. You see, I'm not making myself older like a precocious child. No, getting old for me is just a milestone. I'm putting a notch on the belt a year early for convenience sake. And besides, I just don't care.

I'm at the other end of the spectrum. I figure, what's a year or two among friends? Seventy is a watershed moment when it comes to one's age. I can't change it. I'm not going to say, "Next year I'll be 71." But I may as well be proud of it.

As I alluded to previously, the year before a milestone age is inconsequential, a mere steppingstone—Passover—to history. If someone asks me how old and I tell them that I'll be 70 next year, it steals their thunder. They can't say, "Wow! You're 69? (Say it with me) *Next year you're going to be 70!*"

My family will probably want to throw me a party. They'll make jokes about how, if they put 70 candles on the cake, the smoke detectors would contest the heat and the fire department would show up with axes, hoses, and a Dalmatian.

The firemen would break down the door, stand there in shock, and then say, "Oh, don't tell me it's just birthday candles."

But I understand what's happening here. My window is closing.

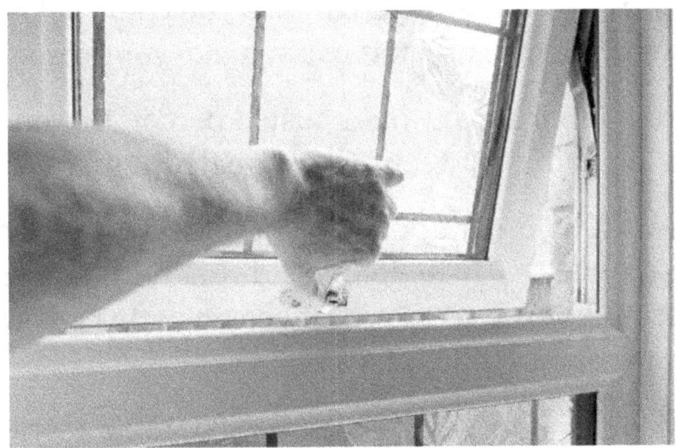

Actually, it closed a long time ago. My desire to make a big splash in a lot of things is pretty much kaput.

At 25 and 30, I thought I could do anything. And there were many things I could have done but I was past my prime. Now I'm a mature being with the experience that comes from being a septuagenarian, without a whole lot of time to do it.

I could still take flying lessons like I did when I was in my twenties. But that notion of flying commercial jets, uh, I don't think so. Some people have a passion early in life and pursue it with vigor. They might receive a push from a parent, but they feed their life's hunger at an early age.

Like Tiger Woods hitting golf balls in the basement with his father at 11 months and competing in tournaments at age five. Eddie Murphy was booking his own gigs at 15. What kind of drive prompted him to do that?

Venus and Serena Williams, coached by their father, began playing tennis at the age of four. And many of the world's most famous comics—Jim Carey, Jerry Seinfeld, Ellen DeGeneres, and David Letterman—all flocked to California just because of the lure of the great Johnny Carson. If you could get booked on the *Tonight Show* back then it could make your career.

What kind of inner force would push a person to want to make audiences laugh in your teens to your early to mid-twenties?

Sometimes life is a conundrum. The fact is, I had visions of becoming a writer early in life but I didn't have the experience to do it. I couldn't run to the coast chasing after a famous talk-show host to make my dreams a reality.

In the back of my mind I may have wanted to be a writer but, in reality, the only writing I did was keeping my resume up to date and working one meaningless job after another.

So here I am. Seventy years of life practice and doing what I am best trained to do.

My desires took time. What can I say? I'm a late bloomer, a guest arriving fashionably tardy for the party.

Throughout this book you've heard me utter the phrase, "I don't care."

Well, there are a lot of things that I don't care about but turning 70 isn't one of them. Age was just a number for every other decade. Every other age road marker except seven-zero hasn't given me much grief.

There's no getting around it, sitting on the cusp of 70 is a butt kicker. Maybe this isn't the way to look at it but in 10 years there's 80.

Eighty is flat-out old; no getting around it.

Old age sucks.

But I'm willing to concede that I'm probably where I'm supposed to be at this stage of my life.

See you at 80—if I should be so lucky.

About the Author

JAMES ROBINSON, JR. is an award-wining author who has written 6 books in both the fiction and non-fiction genres. His first book, *Fighting the Effects of Gravity: A Bittersweet Journey Into Middle Life*, was an Indie Award winner for nonfiction. His first foray into fiction, *Book of Samuel*, was a Readers' Favorite Award Winner. His 6th book—*Jay Got Married*—is a collection of 9 humorous, satirical essays which often speak to ironies and inconsistencies of life.

Jay Got Married is not just the title of the book but the lead essay of the same title and an amusing look at love and marriage in the year 2020.

His latest book, *Old Age Sucks*, currently in the editing stages, could be considered a follow-up to his first book, *Fighting the Effects of Gravity*.

Mr. Robinson began to foster his writing career at age 45 when the Effects of Gravity kicked in and his children began to grow up, affording him the time to write. It was also then that he began to hone in on his sardonic wit.

Mr. Robinson resides in Pittsburgh, PA, with his wife of 43 years. He is the father of three daughters ages 38, 39, and 41 and the proud grandfather of six.

9 798882 559745